The Paper Bridge

The Paper Bridge
Experiential vs. Outdoor Training

JD Roman

libros en red

www.librosenred.com

C.E.O.: Marcelo Perazolo
Managing Editor: Ivana Basset
Cover Design: Emil Iosipescu
Picture of Cover: John Harvey
Interior Design: Federico de Giacomi

Design, typesetting, and other prepress work by LibrosEnRed
www.librosenred.com

ISBN: 1-59754-081-1

First English Edition - Print on Demand

LibrosEnRed©
A trade mark of Amertown International S.A.
editorial@librosenred.com

TABLE OF CONTENTS

Part 1
Introduction and Decalogue

INTRODUCTION

The major project –in terms of budget, scope, and number of participants– of managerial change in Europe took place throughout the years 1995 and 1996, in Chiclana, near Cadiz, in Spain.

20.000 persons from 21 European countries, working with 18 different languages and with OTEL (Outdoor Training Experiential Learning) methodology.

There, during several months, we shared experiences and knowledge with those who would become the main specialist of those skills in Spain (and in other countries as well).

This experience has established a record, in terms of number of participants, diversity of cultures, financial investment, etc.

Taking advantage of the tenth anniversary of the official beginning of the project (March 15 of 1.995), we are going to share some of the knowledge extracted from that experience and from some others which came later.

Well, it is most true that today exist hundreds of companies which offer Outdoors services. Some of them –a few actually– talk about OTEL.

Most of them are lead by pupils of ours, or pupils of our pupils, creating a widespread net of potential suppliers for OTEL sessions. All of our dear alumni are good professionals, but nevertheless we have detected that some ambiguities still remain; ambiguities which feed a permanent debate.

This is a debate which maybe generates something of a "white noise" for the possibly interested clients. In fact, the company clients who are interested in this kind of training face some important doubts, when having to choose a supplier.

The first doubt is: What is this all about, OTEL? What is the OTEL?

And then, obviously, what's the purpose?

The next questions would be: how much does it cost, and what is it going to produce to my company?

Those questions are not innocent. Many companies, attracted by the innovation, have organized for their people jolly good days of rafting, climbing, trekking and others. As well they have organized outdoor days of Paintball, Quads, etc. And so they have spent some serious good time together in the countryside.

But what remains at the end?

A good definition for this kind of sessions comes from a great friend and colleague, one of the major specialists in these matters, Manuel Ferrández. He qualifies them as "The Day of the Tortilla".

The Day of the Tortilla could be described as an event where we gather a bunch of people, move them to a bucolic place, and invite them to take part in a serie of playful activities.

There they are injected with a serie of concepts and company terminology, and ... back home, with a nice tan, a few kinks in the neck and legs and the recollection of having spent a good moment.

And, in fact, the result of those days uses to be always positive. The participants spend it nicely; they reduce stress, they establish some bonds of colleagueship, and always discover something about themselves. But, do those results compensate the carried out expense?

Let's start analyzing then, to discover what OTEL actually is, what's hidden behind those so fashionable terms.

Wishing to document to the max, I have tried to find professionals who before the year 1.995 had developed projects of OTEL in Spain, in order to share with them knowledge and experiences. Not having found any, I am going to try to fix some seminal dates.

At the end of 1.994, we began with the preparation of the Project in Switzerland and United Kingdom (cradle of the OTEL). In March of 1.995, the project began in Spain, in a center specifically designed in the bay of Cadiz, on an area of 20 acres.

So, taking in consideration all of the above we could say that March of 1.995 might be considered as the official date of the appearance of the OTEL in Spain.

From then on, these are the reflections, reflections extracted from experiences and later conversations with the pioneers in Spain, big professionals and great people, with whom I am very honored to continue collaborating.

I have tried to give room to the different nuances –and/or personal interpretations– which have been appearing in the recent years. For that reason, you will notice that in some cases, I express the same concepts but using different formulations, to give some room to all of those nuances.

As well, you will notice that I also try to give some room to concepts like active learning, dynamic learning, effective learning and so on, as all of them are somewhat related.

A historical photo, from the heroic times. A quite unusual experience at that time, where a whole company, from chairman to car washer, participated in a two days OTEL program. Unusual as normally we will want to have homogeneous groups, easier to handle as they share a common "language". On the top left of the image, standing, Antonio Chaves, Eva, and the author. On the top right, standing, Isabel Rey; and, kneeling, Fernando Rodriguez.

At the end of the book, I have included some examples of complex exercises –or rather said, rich of education– though relatively easy to put into practice.

Especially, the Paper Car, the Fall of the Egg, and the Paper Bridge. These three activities, the last one of entirely own design, are my favorites.

With a very small cost (which I detail), they allow us working with groups from a dozen of persons up to 150 persons simultaneously (we name it then the Paper Truck). Though in 2.004, we simultaneously constructed 4 paper cars, in a small bullring (it was a group of 450 persons).

Actually, some of those activities can be performed indoors instead of outdoors (depending on the weather).

The most demanding in terms of time is the Paper Car, which needs approximately three hours to be completed.

The most demanding exercise in terms of facilities is the Paper Bridge, as it requires two couples of trees (or columns of concrete) separated by 5 or 6 meters more or less, and with roughly one meter between each tree.

The Fall of the Egg is a classic exercise in some engineers schools, as a playful activity and a contest for graduation ceremony. Our personal approach is slightly different, although the frame looks very similar.

So, in terms of pedagogic concepts richness, as well as in terms of diversity and depth of metaphors, these exercises represent an appropriate climax for an OTEL without high events (that is, with low cost).

For that reason, at the end of the book, I dedicate a small illustrated chapter to each of them.

So let's begin... But first of all, when we talk about Outdoor and about OTEL, here is my personal Decalogue.

The Decalogue

When I have to train OTEL trainers, I never let them leave my training facility and start working with a group until this Decalogue is deeply ingrained in their minds and turns out into a reflex, whatever the circumstances and the tentative difficulties they may face during the program they are to conduct.

1. OTEL "attacks" the center of emotions, to allow absorptions of reasoned knowledge.
2. The Outdoor is only a subset of OTEL Learning. As well, the activities of Adventure are a mere subset of the Outdoor.
3. The OTEL Learning forces you to move out of the comfort zone to "experience" things, to extract metaphors and to translate them into real life situations.
4. If I do not move, even just a bit out of my comfort zone, I have not learned anything.
5. Every person has a comfort zone of different size and shape.
6. The Outdoor is not a sports contest. You must never lead a participant to his zone of panic.
7. The result of the OTEL programs is not proportional to the cost of the facilities used.
8. The poorer the material we use, the easier the analogies with real life.
9. I avoid "binary" activities, where the result can only be YES or NO (some paradigmatic examples are

the bungee jumping o parachutism, which are not OTEL).

10. I will avoid too long previous explanations. I will allow people to experience, and after the exercise, I will plunge deeply into the analysis (the debriefing).
11. I must combine "frustrating" activities with "rewarding" activities ". This way the analogy with real life is reinforced.
12. I assume that I will never manage to motivate all of the components of a group. What I will have to do is "freeze" the "toxic" components.
13. The most spectacular activities are not the most dangerous. I will have a lot of care with "innocent" activities due to the state of excitement generated in the participants.
14. If I do not do a follow-up to a program of this type, the results can even be counter-productive.
15. The OTEL works always, independently of the composition of the group. The only thing that differs is the richness of the extracted learnings.
16. I will be careful with the cultural differences. The shape and size of the comfort zone has also a strong cultural component. A North American group will probably have a Zone wider than a group of Europeans.
17. The OTEL activities are natural energizers. But even music (Indoor) or activities called "batteries loaders" are also good energizers.
18. The OTEL serves to develop attitudes, but also to prepare to the absorption of "technical" aptitudes.
19. I insist on a correct managing of the time.
20. I ensure that the activities are conceptually supported.
21. Never judge, don't ridicule
22. Careful preparation of the topics and their logistics (one a many causes of failures).

23. Be able to ask, answer and synthesize.
24. I will not use OTEL for purposes opposed to the development of the persons. Handled evilly, OTEL can be a very dangerous tool of manipulation.
25. Always, I will have in mind this Decalogue, when designing and performing OTEL programs.

In this book, we will use indistinctly Outdoor and OTEL, since for us they are the same thing.

The Outdoor being a mere subset of OTEL, although promoting and emphasizing the raw emotional aspects.

As a final word of introduction, ultimately, everything in these techniques is about the acquisition of skills (attitudes and aptitudes) to help us becoming more efficient.

It has nothing to do with a nice picnic weekend.

Part 2
A trip thru OTEL

A MORE DEMANDING COMPETITIVE
ENVIRONMENT

So, the first question would be: Why, as a businessman or manager, do I have I to invest in this kind of methodology?

Obviously, this book is not about management strategy, as we do not pretend to impose our personal point of view about what we think is the "ideal" company. That would be preposterous and arrogant. That's not our objective.

Our objective is to present and discuss some educating, training and skills development techniques which can be used in order to empower a group of people or an organization, whatever the specialty and size of the latter.

We live in times of major changes and transformations. This implies the great responsibility of opening our mind for new options and "unlearning" much of what we have learned, although never forgetting the past.

But, somehow, as not all of the solutions are in the tradition, it is necessary to invent them.

In the particular case of the organizations, given the new rules of the market worldwide, the traditional models of administration and management, designed to handle the existing complexity, are not a response for producing change.

It is necessary to move beyond the burocratic organizations, rigid and dependent, to rely on efficient, productive, flexible and self-conscious organizations where what really matters is the people.

And actually, OTEL has to deal with people, empowering them in order to empower the whole organization.

But, first let's go back to some classic concepts.

Structural change

The complex organizations orientated to the product and with closed borders, will have to turn themselves into opened and interdependent systems, in organizations market-orientated, in which leaders understand that for a space to be gained in the society and to survive, it is necessary to take in account the intentions of its members. For that, pure classical skills are not sufficient.

There is a responsibility of the organization for offering its clients excellent products and services of ideal quality in relation with the price they pay for obtaining them.

Quality helps us remaining on the market, but does not necessarily guarantee the success.

Let's remember that reaching the satisfaction of the client implies just matching his expectations, but if we want to achieve customer loyalty, we need to overcome them.

And to overcome those expectations using the resources we presently have. Those resources –simplifying to the max– could be listed as financial, facilities and human resources.

But the situation is not so simple. It exists a difference between the theoretical resource and the real resource (that is, the outcome I can produce with it).

The technique, the software and the "managerial models", among other things, have created a situation where the persons exceed or are seen as just a mere resource.

One forgets that the concept of effectiveness (to do what has to be done) is not enough. It is necessary to take in account the human being in order to obtain optimum results (to be efficient).

Let's analyze a bit... Returning to the basics (well, basics now we all know...).

DIRECTION VS. LEADERSHIP

The process of management gets lost in the managing of the external and internal complexities. The urgent thing occupies the first place in the to-do tasks and becomes the management rule. We tend to forget the important things or consider them as urgent (when actually no relation whatsoever exists between the urgent and the important tasks)

As well, the pressure caused by not being able to deal with change, limits the possibility of exercising a real labor of leadership.

The traditional manager who decides objectives and tasks to be performed, defines and assigns resources and elaborates budgets, organizes and delegates thru the structure, forms teams (well, actually, groups of people, a team is something different altogether) and executes tasks, and controls (he checks reports, he organizes meetings and solves problems), is not adapted for producing change.

He gets involved in more and more complexity, though no paradigm is broken. We just continue working the way we always have been working, only with much more pressure and stress.

Currently, the top management is perceived as the brain of the organization, forgetting that the organization is a brain in itself. The top managers use the persons for satisfying their own needs and they turn into obsessive persons about control and results.

Additionally, they sometimes get trapped in a classical "clash of titans" and end up just worrying for maximizing their own well-being.

It is necessary to abandon the processes of centralized planning and the paternalistic schemes which generate dependence and erode the internal environment of the organization, reducing the possibilities of human development, reducing his level of commitment and his interest for really taking part in the life of the organization. We cannot continue separating the organization between those who think and those who act.

LEADER VS. MANAGER.
AN OLD DEBATE

The leader, on the contrary, must decide about vision, values, directives and criteria, with the participation of the people, in order that they are the persons and the teams who develop their own plans and take the control of their destinies.

The leader must communicate as widely as possible the necessary information, and he must also qualify and support his people, in order to get them mobilized towards the achievement, eliminating all the interferences and creating spaces for the self-motivation.

Finally, he must guarantee that things happen and do a permanent follow-up of the processes, never failing in recognizing the importance of the flexibility to reach the results.

The leader has to influence his collaborators in order that their potential and energy are use to the maximum for their own benefit and for the benefit of the whole organization.

It is a question of "tuning" the minds of the persons towards a vision and a few common intentions and not on basing the scheme on the simple obedience, since this can turn out to be effective, but not efficient.

And in the competitive environment we are living, I must obtain more with less, and this means being efficient.

Of another hand, he –the top manager– must be able to handle the chaos and the uncertainty in order that the organization survives.

He will have to learn from the crises and from the mistakes in order to continue ahead, provided that the processes of change are not linear but cyclical.

He has to be also intuitive and inspiring, since he will have to be prepared to assume risks and to defy permanently his already deeply ingrained suppositions and paradigms and those of his people. Common sense and simplicity are fundamental for confronting the challenges of the future.

Well, so far everything is just fine, and all of us more or less agree with those basics. But we must analyze more in depth.

How does this relate to training methodologies?

First, remember that between top management and basic staff, there is an extremely important link, the mid management, who is in charge of transmitting to their subordinates, trying not to alter the top management message, though taking in account the specific of each of their collaborators. Not that easy to be achieved. It is a skill which may naturally come, but most likely we will have to learn and practice it.

THE PROCESS OF FACILITATION

The mid-level management is lost in the process of control. The countless areas in which they are in two places at the same time, the traditional organizations and the high number of hierarchy levels, product of the scheme of delegation and control, produce some misunderstandings between top management and their collaborators, causing the mid management to get trapped between both, and thus forgetting their function of "belt transmission".

Additionally, they have the habit of being isolated because of the level of specialization of their functions, for what they must assume individually the pressures and unsuitability of the system.

In the organizations of the future, based on processes defined starting from the needs of the clients and consumers, the mid-level management will be doomed to re-define its role or disappear. Today we already know of companies with just three levels –lean management–, where a "supervisor" can have up to two hundred persons under his responsibility.

When the organizations evolve towards the self-guided teams, where those will be responsible for the organization and planning of their tasks, for the quality and the productivity of their labor, for the managing of the inputs, for their own results, and even, for functions like elaboration and control of the budget, selection of their new members, managing of the assets, discipline, even salaries and relation with the internal and external suppliers, the mid-level management will have to be able to deal with its facilitators role.

Problem is, that role is a new one altogether, and maybe they don't have the skills which will allow them dealing with those new environment parameters. Il becomes mandatory to develop and train new attitudes and skills.

And that cannot be achieved thru classical methodologies. We are talking of a quantum leap in the approach of company business and people management.

A MODEL OF SELF-RESPONSIBILITY

Probably, not every person and team responsible for their own performance and self-control, are fit for the role of "supervisor", therefore our responsibility as managers will be in giving the necessary support, the information and the sufficient resources to guarantee the coherence, the efficiency and the performance of the organization.

As you can see, we establish a total difference between attitude and skills.

This way we come to one of the characteristics into which we will go deeply when we consider OTEL activities OTEL. The notion of self-responsibility.

In French they say "la prise en charge personnelle", hard to properly translate in English, but somehow it tells us that one of the ways of being more efficient, is that the labors of responsibility and individual control are assumed by the actual member of the company

So far, nevertheless, it is habitual that the collaborators, who must assume the responsibility for the achievement, are lost in wilderness.

They may have the attitude, but they don't know what to do with it.

The transformation of the organizations is done fundamentally transforming the persons. The collaborators are actually our main competitive advantage and therefore they deserve the major attention.

So we want to help people experience, understand and finally put into practice that attitude. You understand this cannot be achieved the old way, just telling them to change their attitude. Why? Quite simple, because the organization is not designed that way.

Usually, when a person manages to occupy a position, he faces a quite rigid and mechanized description of the job, with manuals of functions and procedures, standards, relations of authority and controls which limit the possibility of using his talent and intelligence in benefit of the objectives of the company.

But, actually, the flexibility in the above-mentioned elements is an indispensable condition in the process of achievement expected from the collaborators.

We suggest starting thinking about responsibilities and roles in order that every person and every team can handle their environment and find the space where they can increase their productivity and positively impact on the organization.

In this new scheme the structure is not critical. Neither is the approach. We dissociate the people from the structure, so they can be more flexible.

Nevertheless, first of, we must not forget that personal development is all very fine, must that development must serve the objectives of the company an d be consistent with its mission.

In order for the persons to self manage their results, it is necessary to guarantee maturity, commitment and tuning to the vision, the values, the directives and the criteria fixed by the organization.

So it is not so relevant what but why, to allow to the persons to contribute to improvement and change.

The Empowerment

When we talk of "prise in charge personnelle", some authors talk of empowerment. This will change so radically the way of understanding the organizations and the human work that maybe the companies which do not assume it will not survive in the future.

The empowerment does not pretend to give power to the people; it just pretends to not taking it out from them. Once having admitted that the persons "can" and have talent we will stop seeing them as a mere resource or commodity and we will start understanding that their responsibility is to generate resources and add value to the company.

Empowerment, means then, eliminating the dependence and inflexibility of the organizations and its structures, considering and valuing the human being and empowering them in terms of learning and experience.

Empowerment, also means giving options. Common sense tells us that when we give options to a collaborator, he may always choose the more convenient for him, but if he is compromised and desires the organization to be "healthy", he will have to coincide with that is most convenient for all of us.

The insecure managers (namely the non-leaders) or with little power (managers of mid and low level) possibly do not recognize this "power" in the people and are afraid of losing "control" of the situation or of the organization.

Therefore, they waste high amounts of energy supporting the system and status quo, denying the possibility of exploring new ways of exercising the authority. One forgets that the real leaders are not those who are chosen by decree but those who are so recognized by the persons.

In this new conception of the organization, where the principal potential are the people and their intelligence, we must "allow" them to use their talent.

Definitively it is necessary to rethink over the organizations when willing to introduce these new ideas.

But rethinking is not necessarily launching a revolution. Rethinking means having new eyes for the situation.

And, with those new eyes, new methodologies.

With those new eyes, we see that the roles come first, way ahead positions. As well, teams are to be the norm and not the exception. So there is a synergy which breaks the hierarchies and the dependence, where the procedures are replaced by criteria and where we achieve the human growth through the productivity of the whole organization.

Great achievement if we could really walk that path.

The classic approaches of management, "mechanistic", have reached their limits. The Japanese, when talking about North Americans say that those have achieved the "systematized stupidification of production".

Quite harsh, actually, but don't dismiss it too quickly. Remember what happened with the Japanese years ago, then the Koreans, etc ...

But don't let us get fooled by such a nice statement. We must walk that way, but the road is winding and uphill, as it implies we deal with people in a different way altogether. We talk about widespread loyalty, of permanent commitment, end so on ...

In this new scheme, the loyalty is multiple, it relates to clients, teams, chiefs, suppliers, and shareholders.

The way of supporting the system is thru the organizational culture, thru the creation of real commitment in the people, thru communication and thru collaboration.

Only the collaborators with an integral vision of the organization and his environment can contribute and add value. And who is supposed to give them that integral vision?

Everything about OTEL has to do with that.

"Simply" to make people experience, understand, and integrate that challenge.

The immobile trip

The real trip of discovery does not consist in looking for new lands, but in looking with new eyes. This, I believe was said by Marcel Proust, who did not have to move from his armchair to explore new worlds.

What we are talking about is to look for new solutions for old problems.

The organizations are increasingly exposed to confronting new challenges and challenges, for which they must invent their own process and follow a natural and authentic way distinct from the managerial "modes" which have created so many confusion over the past decades.

If I do not change, I may encounter some stability, but actually what I'm facing is downright stagnation, and, provided that the world is in permanent process of transformation, the option is clear.

It is thru embracing change, learning to live with it, and understanding that change is the only real constant in the world. We must demythologize it and, finally, create it.

It is not a question of giving the canvas a few superficial brushstrokes, as the situation demands something more profound.

To achieve it, the principal obstacle I must overcome is the resistance to change.

That resistance comes from the fear we perceive in the top management.

There, courage is needed to confront the adventure of change and the conscience that, by doing what we always have done, we will always get the same outcome.

So, we will have to break paradigms. And well have to do it thru emotions instead of thru reason, experimenting what happens when I explore new lands. That's the explanation of "OTEL".

Though, we are not talking about revolution; it is not necessary to discredit everything that has allowed us to reach current success.

Nevertheless, every organization, assessing their own situation and their vision of future, will have to know if the hour of change has come.

The real social revolution, the one which seeks to improve the quality of life of its members and to maximize the well being, can succeed if we re-define the world of business, of the organizations and of labor.

A sports metaphor

I want to propose the football metaphor –or the basketball, taking advantage of commentaries from my colleague Alfonso Sagi-Vela, whose name is well known in the elite world of basketball–. Though, as what I like is football (well soccer, actually), I am going to translate it in soccer terms.

Let's imagine ourselves –as top managers– yelling instructions to the trainer thru remote control without being in the field, not knowing the skills of the players, but appearing only at the moment of maximum penalties, just to put some pressure on.

Distributing the power between the directors of the "divisions", forwards, midfield, etc...

So, let's think about a captain of football who does not "sweat the shirt" with the team, with partial information and giving orders permanently.

Let's imagine also a forward playing with a "description of job", manuals of functions and standards, and asking for an official permission prior to trying to score.

Will it be possible for a football team to reach success dutifully following a previously established plan? Or presenting "progress reports", and with a permanent institutional audit?

What would be of a team of football if there were no tolerance during the exercise and no aptitude to learn of the mistakes during the trainings?

What happens when we do not know our people and therefore do not offer them the possibility of actually contributing to the overall achievement?

Finally, it is necessary to clarify that it is not a question of anarchy. In football exist rules and values which must be fulfilled. Equally, there are tactics, strategy and criteria for reaching success. The permanent preparation and the trainings are vital and the trainers play a preponderant role inside the team. We have no doubt about the righteousness of all the above-mentioned rules, but can't we give them a slight switch?

Sport shows us that there exist other ways of understanding the organizations and the teams and, that, thru them; the awaited results can be reached. Let's think about them...

But who wins eventually?

The basic point is to understand that the organization, thought as an invention of man, has managed to transform the humanity and the conception of man and work, for what we must look for the possibility that man realizes his own fundamental transformation thru the interaction at work with other human beings.

Sounds pretty philosophical, but that's the way things are, at least from our modest point of view.

Focusing this effort on the clients will be the only thing which will allow the organizations to survive in the future and to achieve the innovation and the creativity that Change increasingly demands.

With this, one expects to fulfill the fundamental objectives, both for the organization and for the persons and the society in general.

Only the companies who talk about culture of change and which support an innovator spirit will be able to be prepared for a more arduous and competed labor caused by the pressure of the markets and of the competition.

So far, so good, but let's move on.

Practical application

Let's see some points, which we will have to keep in mind or to practice when we do OTEL activities.

The typical organization has a rigid boss, and an atomization of the human activity.

The strict control of all the conducts is the underlying principle which inspires it. The dependence and the obedience keep them united.

The stratification and the status symbolize the authority.

The territoriality and individualism give the sense of belonging. It is a complex structure designed to satisfy the needs of the bosses, not the needs of the company.

But survival –prior to the development and growth– of the organizations depends fundamentally on three key protagonists:

The consumers, the key to success.

The shareholders whose satisfaction for the achievements will inspire them supporting or not the assignment of their resources.

The personnel, whose aptitude to attract the consumer and to give simultaneously an added value will guarantee survival in the long run.

Naturally, to re-design the organization towards the consumer leads to new elements to being valued, new skills to being acquired, new internal relations to being established, new tasks to being developed and, finally, to be organized in a different way.

When using OTEL, we will translate these concepts into exercises, and, by the way of metaphors (this is a key word), we will allow the participants to understand what is expected from them back at the workplace.

So, we are implicitly talking about activities which help us learning and integrating skills.

The companies en route for transformation actuate as a system opened to support the harmony between what they do internally and what they achieve in their environment.

Those are organizations which adapt themselves to the variations in the environment and are not mere mechanisms which work without any capacity of response to these variations.

Those companies are organized for the achievement of a vision which unifies and compromises everybody.

They clearly define their criteria of success; they share, apply and respect a philosophy of work, which, according to their belief, is basic for achieving the implementation of the behaviors which eventually lead them to success.

They create mentality of total quality and constant improvement and change their structures orientating them towards the consumer

They reduce levels of authority –lean management– in order to improve the integration and to diminish dependence; they modify the role of the controllers and of the workers in order to increase their capacity of response.

FROM MANAGEMENT TO LEADERSHIP. FROM EFFICIENCY TO PERFORMANCE.

Naturally transformation needs leaders. Persons capable of summoning the energy of others and orientating them towards the achievement of common aims.

The leader is a creator of futures. He knows that the achievement of ambitious goals guarantees the survival of the system and its future development and growth.

The managers, overwhelmed by the weight of the whole Company on their shoulders, multiply their actions, but are they correctly aimed?

They assume the principal role in the company and in the middle of the uncertainty and the increasing difficulty of the future; they concentrate in few hands the key responsibilities.

The members of the Company ask for leadership and it is a responsibility of the management to provide it.

So comes the redefinition of the role of direction and the urgent need to rescue the skills of leadership.

Empowerment at all levels. The "Prise en charge".

The monopoly of the power in the hands of a few hampers the capacity of the great majority to assume responsibilities, to exercise them, to commit themselves with the obtained results and to create a system of constant improvement of the skills and knowledge which would be reflected in an increasing degree in the contribution of every individual and with it, in the permanent development of the company.

Actually, giving responsibilities doesn't mean abandoning areas of actual power. It means delegating what can be delegated, that's all. Getting rid of activities where my added value is irrelevant, and concentrating on actual added value activities. That's a dramatic transformation, for sure.

The transformation ensures that every employee is a living cell of the managerial organism and acts with full capacity in the development of the function to be accomplished.

This is in contraposition to the traditional vision of every employee as a piece of gear, moved by other pieces, rigid, unremovable and blind all of them.

The survival of the company is a responsibility for all its members. The multiplication of the capacity is born from the utilization of the multiple capacities of all the members.

The flexibility relies on that every cell handles the complexity inherent to its function.

STRATEGIC THINKING AT ALL LEVELS. NOT ONLY AT TOP LEVEL

When going OTEL, all levels are involved and committed.

So it seems to be suitable that the leaders have a strategic plan to continue.

Also it seems to be suitable that every position develops its own plan for the fulfillment of the company strategies.

As well, the achievement of success does not depend necessarily on the strict follow-up of the plan, but on the opportune utilization of the favorable options which are appearing and on the overcoming of the natural blockades which arise in the way.

In the OTEL, we will create some artificial blockades, in order to experience. Once again, we will seek analogies with sports, in order to simulate business situations.

A sports star is someone who supports the basic plan with a high dose of skill and ingenuity to create unforeseen plays and to destabilize the scheme of the competitor.

Because of it the OTEL emphasizes so much in the team as basic factor of efficiency.

Administration of change, understood as a constant process

Einstein said: One of our major madness, as human beings is to think that continuing doing things the way we always did, the final results could be somewhat different".

The inflexibility of the organizational structures lead to believe that the possibilities of the organizational change were limited to making more or less of the same thing, to emphasizing or not a procedure or a process, to getting new clients for the same product or new products for the same clients and to introducing just minimal and imperious technological enhancements.

All of this preserving to the maximum the current structure in order to avoid resistances to change and "do not touch" personal interests.

It seemed that the ideal thing for the human beings was the "status quo" in the system of the organization.

If we add systems of planning and of management based on modest increases on historical results, the traditional organization seems to be condemning itself to repeating the script and to hoping that new winds will bring new opportunities, so it doesn't have to be adapting its own structure.

Today the companies immersed in a process of transformation know that the human being associated with others, dutifully organized and with the suitable resources, is capable of ambitious goals.

They understand also that different aims and circumstances need different and adapted organizations.

Therefore the organization must have the flexibility of adapting to the permanent changes in the environment. The change for them is an unavoidable way of survival and therefore it corresponds to the organization to prepare its own change.

Teamwork. The only way to extract more from what we have.

The human being is especially gregarious. We know that the human being as a whole is capable of big accomplishments. Always we said that we must join efforts in order to multiply results.

Nevertheless, for some strange mechanism derived from the technique, we construct organizations for solitary beings, creating positions and divisions which obstruct the union, and, even more systems of control which diminish the possibilities of a collective contribution on the part of the members of the company.

The integration of the organizational system leads to a viable and logical way for multiplying the efficiency of the company.

The teamwork, thru the processes it combines and the assimilation of roles with high interdependence which bring a new conception of the work, where the intelligent utilization of the individual capacity combines with the collective one, generating teams united by common aims in a system of great interaction which promotes the obtaining result, all of that diminishes the dependence and respects the condition of the man as a social being.

Organizational transformation is the entrepreneurship with major capacity of response to the environmental demands, harmonizing the application of the technique.

It guarantees profitability and growth in the long term and better quality of life for its members.

Organizational transformation, what for?

If we read with clarity the previously described terms of reference, we understand that while an organization does not understand the importance of these elements, while it does not understand that the measurement of the quality is not that much in the processes, the procedures or the standards but the persons, change is not on its way.

Only once we have worked on the persons, stand we a chance of developing efficient and respected procedures and ratios.

This approach, typically OTEL may somehow sound unnatural, as we tend to design processes first, and then we try to make people fit in them. With the not so surprising outcome that it doesn't work that much properly.

The first transformation happens inside the human being. In other words, if there is no change of attitude, the aptitudes remain in the mere acquisition of technical knowledge.

This means that it is necessary to be aware of the importance of the individual transformation and the growth of the persons, in search of an increasingly "humanization of the man" and, consequently, a "humanization of the work".

But, if we don't support an integral approach (person-organization), and we decide to interfere with the implications of the process, it will prove to be have been to put a nice front to a weak structure, which, time given will be ruined irremediably.

And we think that this is a vital point to be aware of. OTEL is no cosmetics; it implies a paradigm shift, with all its consequences.

Nevertheless, it is worth a sentence clarifying that a fundamental element of the transformation is the leadership. It is necessary to change managers into leaders, in order that they, in turn, propitiate the necessary environment for the transformation.

This, together with teamwork, will be the only thing which will give congruity to a process of this nature.

How can we develop this facet?

If the "outdoor" and the "indoor" are adequately combined, big benefits can be obtained.

Though it depends on the pedagogic aims, normally the activity out of the classroom occupies the half of the program. Remember we are not in a picnic session.

In order for this tool to work, we must have a correct approach. There are no standard programs; and every company has different needs so the programs are to be tailor made.

It is necessary to meet with the director of human resources or with the top manager of the company and write together a script, where we write down the improving points.

With this information, we can start working on the de-

A small simple activity. No need for expensive material. You can do it with stones, boxes, or whatever other available material. What's important is that the whole team participates in reaching the highest high (or the together decided highness objective). There is no simpler exercise.

sign of the programs and activities which are going to be developed. With the OTEL methodologies, we want, thru the experience, to foment a change of attitude when it is necessary.

Then, the whole sequence is analyzed in order to correct the mistakes and to promote the strong points of every participant.

Nevertheless, we do not allow the showiness of the exercises to darken the training, since it would be a hobble for achieving the final outcome.

Nonetheless, the activities must be attractive due to the fact that, in some cases, these activities days are celebrated even during the weekend, and the managers must be motivated and predisposed to learn.

At the conclusion of the days, the persons in charge of the company are to make a follow-up of the application of the learned new tools, because in some cases, they may need reinforcement.

The OTEL activities generate situations with a great potential for learning. Nevertheless, we are sorry to see that sometimes during these experiences lived outdoors some groups fail in taking advantage of the created conditions and the whole experience remains a mere amusement –the Day of the Tortilla–, when they are not organized by real professionals in those matters.

Neither it is enough to expose a theory after the activity.

The challenge of a good analysis needs from the facilitator experience and sensibility to detect the richest moments, to analyze the expressed messages, to check in group how the conflicts have been solved, to unveil the unexpected behaviors of the group, to favor that each one thinks upon the experience, and, if necessary, changes attitude.

This is specified not to hurt, just to emphasize the positive thing and to motivate.

To achieve an integral training

The ideal of the OTEL is to obtain an integral training. Not only concepts will be learned –team, dialogue, assertivity, roles...– but skills will be developed –of communication, planning or distribution of tasks–.

"It has to be a learning which touches the inner depth of the person, without being a nuisance, and transforms his attitudes towards the collaboration, the work into team and the value of the individual differences".

What we have learned under an intense emotion, we never forget. Besides, to innovate it is necessary to break with the present environment, without forgetting that our authentic value develops out of the habitual context (namely out of our comfort zone).

Our exercise of the Paper Bridge is a graphical illustration of this classic metaphor in psychology, where two persons meet in the middle of a monkey bridge, swaying over troubled waters, giving to a banal act a tremendous psychological weight, due to the situation of "risk".

It indicates that the teams and the organizations construct themselves more around shared emotions than around rational ideas.

All these practices fit perfectly in programs of development of social skills –especially when a change of attitude is what we look for– and in those who try to obtain a rethinking of the own way of actuating –initiative, confidence, leadership, creativity, communication ...–.

Some fashionable term for defining the above mentioned is Emotional Intelligence (EI). OTEL actually works on the 5 facets of EI.

Also it is very advisable when we seek to improve aspects such as planning, time management, negotiation, intercultural communication, total quality, knowledge management, or when we want to develop skills related to the work in group, multifunctional, self-guided teams, taking of decisions, resolution of conflicts, motivation.

And what's the situation in Europe, and especially in Spain?

Due to a deep-rooted classical model business Spanish culture, it still costs a lot for the businessmen to have confidence in the new methods ... until they try them and they surprise themselves when seeing that the results are positive.

On the other hand, in the northern countries, OTEL is more largely used, as actually the pioneers were located in UK

Luckily, the efficiency of the results with the practices of OTEL, has motivated that some of the most prestigious business schools apply this methodology inside their programs of managers training.

One of the principal aims these schools have in mind is that the participants, in general managers proceeding from different countries and cultures, have the opportunity to contact rapidly and to work as a team since the beginning of the course

Some companies trust fully in the OTEL methodology, in such a way that they include it in the programs of training and development for new managers.

They are programs of six months of duration designed in order that the young personnel acquire the necessary training to be tomorrow the directors.

But beware: The OTEL methodology is not substitute of the classic training.

After a theoretical and more classical training, then we can do OTEL during a weekend for instance.

We, as facilitators supervise the actions of every group, analyze them at their conclusion, and then analyze more in depth the behavior of its members with the intention of correcting the weaknesses and promoting the strengths.

The OTEL is a methodology of existential training consisting of a group of persons who are employed at the same company develop activities in the outdoors.

Nevertheless, we have conducted OTEL, with different companies involved, normally companies linked by supplier-client bonds, who want to work according to Total Quality Management principles, that is, involving the whole added value chain members along the whole business processes.

The activities which will allow us reaching that integration differ in terms of complexity, cost and logistics. The only limits are our own imagination.

For instance, we can think of exercises like constructing a raft to cross a river. One of the objectives is to observe individual and team behaviors.

The correlation is demonstrated between what they do during the activity and how they act in his working place.

The final aim is to develop personal and team skills; that is to modify conducts and attitudes.

What differentiates the OTEL of other methods of education is that the retention and fixation of the learned thing are very high because they are acquired thru a personal emotional experience.

But the OTEL is effective only if what's learned by the participants is translated into company situations. It must not remain in the step of self-knowledge and knowledge of the others: it is necessary to take it back to the working place.

The OTEL has become fashionable and it has provoked that some companies specialists in sports events offer it among their services, though behind the activities there is no an authentic formative aim, but rather mere outdoor games.

We have no problem with that approach; it just serves a different purpose. What we must not do is confusing OTEL and pure adventure.

A PROGRAM OF OTEL
INCLUDES SEVERAL PHASES.

We have to:

To know the needs of the company.

To analyze the aims which the client is seeking to achieve, and to recommend him the best solution.

The OTEL is useful to improve the work in team between departments, to learn how to take decisions with rapidity, etc. It does not serve to solve problems of structure of the company or of its systems of management. Although a change of attitude might be a good starting point for a re engineering of processes.

Defining the pedagogic aims

The program has to be tailor made. It is necessary to orientate the activities towards what we want to be obtained.

Developing the activity and observing the participants

The facilitator sees how they act and he only intervenes and helps them to learn by themselves.

Thinking

Once having finished the activity, what happened is analyzed. The facilitator directs the discussion with questions which are orientated towards the aims of the program and helps by questions and metaphors about the activity.

Reinforcing the learned

A follow-up is performed in order to see how what happened is being translated into the company daily reality.

The same OTEL activity has infinity of possibilities according to the way we orientate it in agreement with the formative aim which has been previously decided.

The facilitator must possess knowledge of organizational behavior, experience in managerial environments and skills of training.

The meetings trainings, with more than one facilitator, enrich enormously the programs of OTEL, although they come to be more expensive.

If activities that are realized outdoors are of certain complexity (rock climbing for instance), specialized facilitators will have to be involved.

The suitable thing is to realize the program in a natural environment, in a place where the participants feel relaxed and disconnect from their routine in the company.

The OTEL is an existential methodology, for what the best way of understanding it is plunging in it.

It develops out of the classrooms thru activities where the participant is the absolute protagonist.

The activities have to be playful for the participants to relax and break inflexibilities, but the aim is to develop skills which can be applied in the company.

Human development is very fine, but we, as managers must ensure that the investment we have made produces concrete results back at our workplace.

Pure Outdoor. But careful with the aspects of Security. The logistics for this activity are quite complex. Not all of the water locations are suitable. We will use it only with small groups and only under extremely strict and professional supervision.

Classic example of exercise of OTEL. The raft

The participants get gathered indoors in a room and the activity is explained: we have to construct a raft and to cross the river from a shore to another and then back.

We are about twelve persons, have about one hour and a half of time and some very rudimentary material to work with.

A specialized facilitator delivers two palets, four tubes of truck tires and two inflating pumps, ropes, scissors and little more. This is not a restrictive list; if you can think of some other material, go ahead. We just don't recommend the use of metal, preferring wood and cardboard.

So the activity begins; it begins quite well, part of the team devotes itself to locating shallow waters in the river, while the rest is inflating the tubes, but at the moment of constructing the boat we start improvising, and problems appear.

This happens often in the companies: an aim is defined but the steps are not planned correctly to reach it, or, worse than that, we lose aim because of the pressure.

So, what normally happens is that we construct two crafts because spontaneously appear two leaders who, without even realizing it start initiating parallel projects.

So we have divided our efforts and the team loses strength. Every time we have performed this activity, we faced this kind of situation; it is a very classical human behavior.

None of the two rafts is technically suitable, but after several attempts we manage to make a person cross the river. Not very aesthetically, merely efficiently (she didn't drown).

Nevertheless, we ran out of time, so we "failed".

Exhausted and dull we return to the meeting point. The "facilitator" helps us thinking about our successes and mistakes as a group.

It is not necessary to point at any culprit: the video of the activity is sufficient for everyone to realize what they have done well and what they have done wrong.

The video session is frankly entertaining: it has its playful part, but it helps us undertaking some serious reflection which serves us to understand the connection which exists between the performed activity and the daily work back at the company.

Though this has been only an exercise and despite the fact that the participants didn't properly work together nor managed to reach the formative aim, we still can see that the exercise has been effective.

Because what emerged from the debriefing was:

The lack of communication, the absence of a single organizing leader, the scanty planning, the form in which some persons take part actively while others remain on the edge, etc.

We observe that these roles are the same we play at our working place and it makes us discover which group attitudes and behaviors can lead to success and which might lead to failure.

Can it work in my company?

For several profiles: professionals who are employed at different physical delegations and do not know each other personally; groups of persons who will join the company shortly and will have to work in team; and heads of different departments of the company.

Those could be some high-priority participants, although it works for everybody.

Few believe that because of the peculiarities of their organization the OTEL could not be a success.

The majority feels satisfied with the experience.

Why? It is clear that they have lived the experience and discovered how much it may be useful for them.

That's why we state that OTEL always works, in a more or less profound way.

They are more and more numerous the companies that day after day use and implement the programs of OTEL, to develop processes of organizational transformation, development of skills, processes of change, etc. The results are interesting at all levels.

Undoubtedly the participants in this experience remain positively marked, with an action plan to turn their weaknesses into strengths.

But, let's deepen a bit. What is all of this about? "OTEL" "training outdoors", "experiential training", "Experiential learning", or "Outdoor Training"? What are the origins?

A LITTLE BIT OF HISTORY

Some say that the "OTEL" was born in 1964.

This, according to some colleagues from Harvard or from Milton Keynes.

I suppose that it is necessary to be a little bit more flexible. Personally, I do not believe that the OTEL was born, let's say, on July 4 of 1.964 in Boston (or in Guatemala City, as far as I am concerned).

The fatherhood of OTEL is not so crystal clear.

Simply, in the 60s many people started being aware of the need for exploring other paths.

In those early years, in many occasions the simulations and exercises implied some actual physical and imminent risk for the participants.

Little by little this figure of risk has been eliminated, developing a serie of safety procedures and special attachments which allow us offering safety to the members of the groups who take part in the workshops.

Certainly this implies a specific training for the professionals, the facilitators and the persons who intervene in this type of courses.

Nowadays, in the OTEL we can find a great quantity of variations with regard to the original idea. There are activities in the water, air or land; many of these can range from the mere game up to the most extreme adventure, such as rowing down troubled rivers in the modality of rafting.

We want to make clear that simplicity in the OTEL does not involve a minor challenge, simply it refer to the logistics (and cost) each of the exercises implies and to the adrenaline they generate in turn.

We will talk later about physical activity and its organic positive impact when having to train adults or children.

But what has to do with business sailing along a river in a raft, being in a very dense forest in search of a track with a compass which will lead us to a meeting point with our colleagues; or walking along a river with bandaged eyes, with the water up to the knees and a colleague working as a guide?

This type of activities, besides being a technique is also a "philosophy", allowing developing the skills the members of an organization need to obtain success.

The exercises are created and designed to develop particular skills, as work in team, leadership, communication, planning, flexibility, initiative, and self-confidence amongst others.

And the whole process consists of four phases:

Experience

Practice

Feedback

Generalization

What we want to make clear if that the activities do not remain simply in games with balls, trunks, etc. We will permanently and heavily insist on that characteristic of OTEL.

One of the most important phases in the process is the feedback, better known as "debrief".

In this step, the experiences of the team are to be translated into application in real life. Also, analogies are realized between what they lived during the activity and what awaits them back at the workplace.

This moment of reflection allows the members of the group to be conscious about future areas improvement.

The great competitive difference of this technique takes root in this simple statement, which all educators well know.

A person learns 20 % of what he sees, 20 % of what he hears, 40% of what he hears and sees simultaneously and 80 % of what he experiences and discovers by himself.

Definitively, here the participant is the one who constructs his learning, the learning being not delivered just as a recipe.

The participants will be interacting with others and they have to take decisions, planning their strategies and assuming the responsibility of what is done or not.

The experiences, besides developing some aspects in the persons, allow in turn consolidating these experiences, creating bonds of friendship, confidence and union which are difficult to break after having faced together such a challenge.

And that's the target we were aiming at. How exciting it is to get there, whatever the specialty of your company, whatever the profile of your people, whatever the cultural background actually.

Nevertheless, we will have to introduce some cultural nuances when developing an OT. A North American audience is quite different from a Spanish audience. Their comfort zones are quite different.

Also, beware with the vocabulary.

Reaching the top. This is Outdoor Adventure. It is not OTEL. Don´t be confused by the complexity (and cost) and risk of the activity. Go for the simplest and quickest to perform. When needed, we can always jump to adventure activities, but only for selected groups. Top right, our adventure specialist, Javier Caballero.

For instance, in Spain, some Spanish companies participate in the Rain forest Trophy, or in the Challenge of the Heights, where several companies compete for a record.

The teams must overcome a serie of exercises where the work in team, the leadership and other skills are fundamental to triumph. But that's another story ...that's not OTEL

This, the extreme adventure, as we say in our Decalogue, is only a subset of the Outdoor, Outdoor being, in turn, only a subset of OTEL.

We are focused on OTEL, not on adventure.

Finally, and somehow summarizing what we have shared so far, OTEL is an advanced tool in the processes of training in the organizations, is a technique and a philosophy we must handle with ethics and professionalism and with a great critical sense of what wants to be achieved thru it.

Let's continue with our trip through the OTEL world.

The managers' challenges

We have seen that leading and managing a company is very complicated. The pressing market, the new products, the persons who shape the organization, the economy and all the internal and external variables influence definitively the development of any business.

So far, so good.

But it exists a definitive variable for the success of the company. A variable which can modify, improve and discover the strong and weak areas. This variable is the person, the Human Being, basically YOU.

So we must ask ourselves some basic questions:

Have you wondered which are your best skills?

Have you all the necessary characteristics to lead a company?

Do you feel you possess skills but have found impossible to develop them?

Do you have internal fears?

What is the level of communication you have with your peers?

Can you work in team?

Are you flexible facing the changes which are generated at all levels?

What is your confidence degree?

What are your plans for the future, both personal and professional?

To all of these questions it is necessary to answer if we want to fulfill what we had dreamed and planned.

We, the human beings, are not accustomed to evaluating ourselves, to asking us things and much less to other persons evaluating our behaviors.

It is complicated to think on oneself and to modify the course we have given to our existence. For nobody it is a secret that it is easier to speak about the others than of oneself.

A real entrepreneur must know likewise how to lead the others and how to establish challenges for himself. There exist many ways of training which allow us to develop and to discover what really exists inside each one.

The power of the OTEL finds its roots in the fact that the person has direct contact with the experience.

It is demonstrated that the experience is learned much better that way, instead of in a classroom.

How does OTEL work? It consists of a series of simulations, exercises and / or activities with missions and specific challenges, designed to exercise and to develop the skills in the persons (always first the attitude, then the skills).

Later, we will devote a whole chapter to effective learning, opposed to repetitive learning

Probably to construct a raft and to sail along a river in search of a specific target is a good team challenge, but not only that, that activity helps us generating emotions which will "open" our person and allow the acquisition of knowledge. Euphoria as a tool for "penetrating" the inner human being.

EMOTIONS AND LEARNING

The emotions which generate these activities are indescribable for the participants. To fulfill a mission marked by an instructor is a real challenge and the satisfaction that one feels on having realized it is a motive of celebration for the whole team.

Other activities are directed to develop confidence in oneself. It is not easy to jump from a platform of wood to another, all installed in a tree 10 meters high, and separated from each other 1 meter approximately.

This is a real challenge. The sensation of emptiness and of fear is present and you are alone.

These moments will help us overcoming our internal fears and discovering the real potential that exists in our interior.

THE FACILITATOR

But the OTEL is slightly more. We need something else apart from the mere activities. We need the facilitator.

The facilitator is the person entrusted to develop the phases of the process in the OTEL.

Every activity, generally, is divided in three parts:

1. The briefing. A serie of instructions which indicates the participants what they have to do, in terms of script of the activity, time, level of the challenge, etc.
2. The process of experiencing the exercise
3. The process of feedback, (the debrief).

This step is even more important than the experience itself. During the debrief it is when everything what happened is commented; and when we share the sensations and emotions.

This leads us, little by little, very finely, to contextualize what was executed, relating it to the daily activity of the persons back at the workplace or at home.

It is very interesting to realize that many of the experiences are exactly equal, or very similar, to those of the daily life.

The persons discover that there exist opportunities to solve problems, and that it is not necessary to look for new horizons, but to look with new eyes.

Others decide to restate their former point of view. Even some of them even distinguish two periods in their lives: "before the process" and "after the process" of the OTEL.

We are talking of very serious statements here.

WHY IS IT SUCH A SUCCESS?

It has been verified that the persons, after receiving classes of magisterial type on a certain topic, realize that, after some time has passed, the recollection of the learned is low.

The OTEL is different because the person is the protagonist of his learning, the decisions that he and his team take are fundamental for the success or the failure of the challenge they face.

We know many people, who, after living through a process of OTEL years ago (ten years is not a problem), remember the experiences and the learnings as clearly as it had happened yesterday.

All of this is quite fine, but how it is possible to apply this program in a company and what can be achieved thru it?

The OTEL applies to obtain specific aims.

Many companies, or groups of persons, decide that they need to learn to work as a team, others think that they need to develop skills of leadership, or to face mergers, or to process some organizational transformation.

In these cases the strategic management of the company is re-defined, as well as the mission, the vision, the values and the principles of organization.

The personnel feel the organization as belonging to all, so the sense of belonging grows and fortifies in them.

Other organizations in the process of change prefer using OTEL for specific purposes.

The process must continue with an internal follow-up in order to extract the major profit and to develop all the ideas of improvement which have been generated. What we identified as the fourth step of OTEL.

But, for achieving all of that, there is a role which has a specific weight, the leader.

Six steps for developing a program. Prerequisites

One of the aspects which marks an important difference between the companies of success, and those which are not successful is the capacity and quality of its leaders.

If we understand the leadership as the art and the process of mobilizing and orientating the whole talent, the commitment and the passion of a human team towards the achievement of common aims, we can see the leadership as a fundamental element of the organization.

Today exists some consensus about how skills of leadership can be developed; the sole difference is in how doing it. The skills are developed putting them into practice (experiencing, once again), not reading or listening.

Thru this process, we seek to detect areas of improvement and strengthening, to develop the critical skills, to generate productive confrontation, to establish commitments and, finally, to realize a follow-up and permanent accompaniment, to assure the application and usefulness of the process, which will be reflected in a better environment of work and better results for the organization.

Awaited results

- To develop visible skills of leadership in the organization.
- To create a culture of leadership based on values, promulgated with the example and centered on the empowerment of the human being.

- To increase the development of the leadership towards better results for the organization
- To affect positively the improvement of the internal environment of work.
- To create innovation, learning and improvement in the organization,
- To orientate the collective efforts towards the achievement of the mission and vision.
- To develop strategic thinking, relations of confidence, commitment and empowerment in the organization, so the leader can develop his facilitator's real role.
- To involve everybody with the commitment of the leader.
- To support a real competitive advantage thru leadership.

Justification and awaited result

Not to rely on real leaders is costlier than to develop them.

Not only because of the impact on the organization, but because of the consequences that a process of this nature produces on the society. Then the need for developing a process of OTEL becomes crucial.

Though the complete results are not seen in the short term, a process which implies commitment, implantation and follow-up, quickly begins to show positive results which justify the effort.

Time given, one expects to reconstruct the organization, to develop a new culture and to achieve a real innovative organization, an organization which learns and improves constantly thru its personnel.

Six steps for developing a program.

We had seen that the OTEL programs contain 4 main phases. We can tune them finer, detailing into 6 steps.

STEP 1: KNOWLEDGE OF THE ORGANIZATION

To be able to orientate adequately the process, we recommend you thoroughly know the organization from within. This implies visits, individual and group interviews as well as the study of the corresponding supporting documents.

STEP 2: KNOWLEDGE OF THE "STATE OF THE ART"

Designed together with the client, to adapt it to the reality and needs of the company, a diagnosis will be realized for global evaluations.

This diagnosis turns out to be a personal and group report, which emphasizes resistances and areas of improvement.

STEP 3: CONFRONTATION AND COMMITMENTS

Thru individual and team meetings, the results are analyzed trying to get commitments from each of the leaders, with their corresponding action plans and follow-up.

STEP 4: CONCEPTUALIZATION

Performing a one-day conceptual session on leadership, to share and to validate knowledge, to link it to the reality of the organization and to the results obtained in the step 3.

STEP 5: THE OTEL

Once obtained the results of the step 3, we will develop an existential workshop designed specially for every case on agreement with the above-mentioned tentative results.

The existential workshop of three days top serves, besides developing skills; to perform tasks related to the Vision, Mission and Values of the organization, the review of commitments, the plan of action and follow-up as well as to define the way of measuring the advances produced during the process.

Step 6: Follow-up

Roughly, 4 quarterly meetings of follow-up should be performed.

The first one consists of individual meetings to check advances and to restate commitments.

The second one is carried out with the whole team, to analyze as a whole what has been developed and to penetrate into topics where still remain possible worries. In this session they will perform some indoor or outdoor exercises, in order to reactivate the emotions they experienced during the OTEL.

The third one implies a new exercise to measure whether the persons of the organization perceive the changes. In this measurement it is possible to decide of a meeting for individual and / or in team feedback.

The fourth and last, is again a meeting with the team to "perfect" (to "tune") the process and to analyze the obtained advances and to define a plan of action towards the future.

It is necessary to observe that from step 1, it is mandatory to design a strategy of communication for the rest of the organization, in order that they are informed of the whats and whys of this process.

Otherwise, there exists a high risk of misunderstanding, and even of rejection. I have heard it many times, especially in Spain or in France, where to the participants, all this stuff looked like nothing else than an "americanada" (freely translated, yanqueeness, or whatever other contemptuous description you could think of) and the final results could even be negative. So be extremely careful with the preparation of an OTEL, but especially with how we present the action to the organization.

When about to presenting the idea to the organization, and to make everybody understand how high the stakes are, we should prepare a statement like this one.

"It is clear that the speed at which today the companies move in their relation with the market and in the professional environment in competition with new companies, mergers, technological innovations is increasing. This demands a permanent effort from the managers in order to be better prepared for the new professional challenges".

"And it may demand a quantum leap in the methodologies to be used".

Undoubtedly among all these challenges we would place in a privileged order question as the correct coordination of teams, the suitable relation with the subordinates or the assumption of the own labor as integral part of a wider group responsibility.

Unquestionable premises which, nevertheless, not always are fulfilled satisfactorily. What to do in these cases?

The OTEL or active training was born precisely to solve this type of questions

An Anglo-Saxon technique

Remember that we already spoke about the birth date of OT, allegedly in 1.964. Well, it's not that simple...

The Anglo-Saxon countries incorporated this methodology not from scratch; they took impulse on the exercises the pilots of the air British forces, who wanted to volunteer during the Second World war, had to fulfill.

Thru the above-mentioned exercises, they wanted to stimulate in the soldiers values as commitment or the capacity of leadership. So we see that the year of official birth is very diffuse.

In its application to the civil world, the methodology consists of a series of exercises in which the managers or personnel learn how to work in team, and how to coordinate efforts and unite criteria.

That is to say, the fundamental aims of this type of training are to help these persons to be able to identify the professional problems, and, especially, to offer some suitable way of solving them.

Obviously, it is no longer a matter of life (the war is over), but the situation in the market demands more and more from the persons.

We are ordinary people living in times of extraordinary changes. Just remember some of the major changes we have endured in just the past decade: Internet, mobile phones, Euro as a common currency in Europe, the treaty of Schengen, and so on...

Once you start thinking over all of those dramatic changes, you realize that you, as a person, have to undergo some major change as well, otherwise, you may get lost, devoured by the frantic pace of acceleration in the business world.

So, same as with our military metaphor, everything starts when a group of professionals –between ten and twenty, chosen by their company– prepares to face, during two or three days a serie of exercises directed to favoring their team spirit, their aptitude to communicate or any other need derived from their professional activity.

We are not talking of "the dirty dozen", don't be so dramatic, but we are talking of a profound experience, not a picnic weekend.

The group coexists during these days in the facilities where the program takes place, sharing emotions so opposed as dread, happiness, tension or uncertainty, and extracting from the exercises the conclusions corresponding to their professional profile.

For example.
Some simple and cheap exercises.

In every course one comes to realize an average of six exercises, where does not intervene the facilitator, who limits himself to observing the way in which the group communicates, how the decisions are taken, etc.

It is then in the classroom —or sat in bare banks of stone— when the facilitator helps them detecting their failures (we should say areas of improvement instead) and strengths. It is the step of the "debriefing".

Among the most usual exercises those of orientation are quite common (and by the way, quite cheap to develop).

With the only aid of a map and a compass, with a time limit, they have to find several checkpoints concealed in a forest.

This labor demands the participants the establishment of a certain strategy. To define the aims, to be exposed to the dependence of other colleagues, etc.

Other exercises among many can be the climbing in group of a climbing wall, more and more easy to find, in schools of climbing, even in some universities. Quite cheap to rent actually. Problem can be the logistics, if the local facilities are not rich enough for developing other OTEL activities.

Also, the construction of a raft with logs, tubes, and ropes. Cheap, but demanding some special security features. Remember what we said about it.

Another one, very effective and cheap, is the so-called ski race, where the complete team, standing on two parallel planks, must advance in a coordinated way (otherwise, the stumble and fall are guaranteed).

Nevertheless, whatever the exercise, the key of the process is that the exercises and the theoretical reflection are very closely related.

Because of it, whenever they finish an exercise, the participants gather with the facilitator, who makes them see the relation between the exercise and their daily work, the reason why the exercise has not been OK or why it has properly functioned.

As you notice, it is not that relevant for the exercise to be a "success". Remember, we are not talking of a sport contest.

Many times, we learn much more from our failures than from our successes. What we want is to open the eyes of the professionals to difficulties in they labor routine; difficulties they could not manage to detect, and obviously even less overcome.

Beware nevertheless. In order not to generate too much frustration, the facilitator must be top level and very well aware of how to deal with frustrations; otherwise, the results can be extremely negative.

We can see that the cost cannot be a major impediment for doing OTEL. If our budget is low, we can decide to use cheap activities. The results will nevertheless be outstanding.

So, as always, a sensitive point is the costs. The fees can range between the 4.000 and 6.000 $ for a program with a total duration of two days, where intervenes a group of fifteen participants.

What will mark the difference is the complexity of some activity (there are some of them which turn out to be very expensive) and the "cachet" of the facilitator. I know that when I contract some colleagues of mine, I have to multiply the final price at least by two.

Nevertheless, sometimes it compensates me to bring a guru. Never forget that although the exercises by themselves are very powerful, you must select your facilitators with great care.

Also, this is also a factor of motivation; the fact that the facilitator is a renowned figure, contracted specially for this program.

It is a question, nevertheless, of approximate fees. It is necessary to stand out the fact that, when having courses designed specifically for every need, the cost of the courses can change notably depending on the circumstances and the concrete aims of every case.

Anyway, our message could be that money cannot be an insurmountable obstacle when willing to do OTEL.

METHODOLOGIES

Let's see now where the OTEL fits in a more global process of development.

Man examines concepts to rethink them and, hereby, to incorporate them into his daily practice, if he considers them of usefulness.

Starting from the objective of the learning: "To promote the participant for a better performance from the acquisition and learning of new knowledge, new skills and therefore new attitudes".

Concretely, for the adult, the objective is to apply the above-mentioned knowledge in his family, social and labor role.

By virtue of the above paragraph, it is clear that for the construction of that knowledge, we need experimentation (hence the word OTEL) ... therefore, any learning should begin with the practice and application of the skills, the knowledge and the attitudes necessary for a certain roe or position.

They are precisely the active (where we include Outdoor and OTEL) methodologies of training which make a more rapid approximation to learning, since they allow us interacting since the beginning with the subject, with the above mentioned object of knowledge, making possible reflection conceptualizations and experiences which lead to effective changes.

So let's have a look at the conceptual and methodological foundations, as well as at some strategies for their implementation.

ACTIVE METHODOLOGIES

A definition might be "Set of educational actions systematically organized to guarantee knowledge thru the direct participation of the subjects on the same educational act".

The essence itself of the active methodologies is the performance and direct experimentation of the participant with OTEL and learning activities.

The active methodologies in the managerial education claim that the adult assimilates and learns how to achieve an extraordinary performance (the famous efficiency).

It is important to bear in mind that the active methodologies obey the logics of the Formative Model of learning, referring to the combination of both physical and mental activity, looking for the correct balance, in order to construct or develop some skills.

Otherwise, again we are facing a jolly "Day of the Tortilla".

The OTEL is a style of educational intervention where the participant plays an active role thru his personal self-determination and the conscious development of actions to transform reality.

The facilitator of the process accompanies him thru the experience, reflection and conceptualization, guiding him towards the extrapolation to his personal and labor life.

In order to enrich the OTEL approach, and more specially in the field of adults training, there are diverse theories we can find in the way, especially in the last years where this methodological trend has caught strength among the facilitators of educational processes.

The OTEL, besides being more than a tool, is a Philosophy of education for adults. It initiates from the principle that the persons learn better when they enter in direct contact with their own experiences. It is learning by "doing".

It is necessary be careful with how we use the word Philosophy, which can sound as some kind of not very practical and to the ground reality.

This modality does not limit itself to the sole exhibition of concepts, but thru the accomplishment of exercises, simulations or dynamical activities, search that the person assimilates the principles and puts them into practice, developing his personal and professional skills.

But, what is that inner process? What happens inside the participants´ hearts and souls?

Learning process in the OTEL education

Starting at a need felt and/or expressed by the one who learns, the learning process achieves a major efficiency if bearing three steps in mind:

Awareness, Conceptualization, Contextualización based on the OTEL for reaching a suitable balance in the assimilation of information.

1. CONSCIENCE

By means of experiences and exercises the participants are aware of all the cognitive, affective and behavioral options in relation with the select topic. This first step is based on the existence of both cerebral hemispheres which intervene in the learning. One of them, the right, is driven by experiences and not by theoretical reasoning. A person learns from his own needs and experiences, and if a theory he listens or reads is not related to the above-mentioned needs and experiences, he will not learn it. The accomplishment of a dynamics or exercise in this phase, comes followed by an individual and group reflection on the experience, in order to analyze, to determine priorities and to share reflections; to listen, to value and to evaluate themselves or others; and to choose options.

2. Conceptualization

By means of a theoretical and practical confrontation, the persons evaluate their reality, formulate and exercise a congruent model of action. Theoretical concepts are shared to authorize the language, facilitating to better understand the experiences. The incorporation of this step departs also from the existence of both cerebral hemispheres which intervene in the learning; the left-handed, learns with theoretical reasoning. A learning based exclusively on experiences and lacking of a theoretical frame which gives it a rational logical explanation, tends to be quickly forgotten.

3. Context

The participants apply and translate the topic object of study to their labor and personal reality, in order to design plans of action and self-evaluation, looking that every person contacts with himself, with his own reality and with his participation in the achievement of results. Assuming that what is not practiced is not learned. Besides, a real learning is the one which changes the conducts or way of life of the person.

Inside the active methodologies exist diverse types of methods or models, although they all spin around the same basic concepts.

OTEL

Literally, the term OTEL means "training out of the doors" or, training in opened field. It recounts to the activities of OTEL which are executed in open field, out of the zone of work, even out of the zone of physical influence of the organization. But moreover, out of the comfort zone (which, remember, is not a physical Zone, the comfort zone is a mental Zone)

It deals with overcoming basically a series of obstacles which eventually represent certain aspects of the managerial and personnel life of the participants.

INDOOR TRAINING (AS PART OF THE OTEL)

"Training indoors". It consists of the application of a series of simulations by means of practices in closed spaces, generally inside the organization. The processes of training Indoor tend to use also the OTEL as central methodology of the educational process.

ACTION REFLECTION PLANNING

Learning process which, from action, takes the individual to a confrontation with real thing to produce an imbalance thru the experience itself. This allows him or her to think, to analyze and to take decisions to "plan" adequately, (or at least better), on the short term.

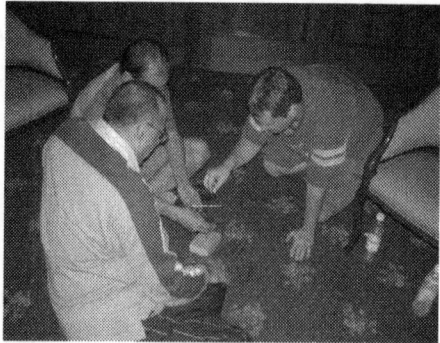

Small indoor activity. As you can see, no need for expensive material or facility. What's important is that the group shares a common project.

COMFORT ZONE ZONE OF LEARNING

This methodology proposes to move from a comfort zone to a zone of uncertainty –or learning–, which produces knowledge. While the individual remains in a frame of comfort or safety, without risking to live and experiment, to interchange, to interfere with other processes, to face other persons or other realities, it is very difficult to extend his comfort zone and to acquire new knowledge.

To overcome the dread implies certain breaks and inconveniences which produce discomfort and imbalance. At the moment the person moves and risks new experiences, that person is opened to absorbing sensations, reflections and eventually, to new knowledge. The aptitude to make participant agree to go out or not of the comfort zone it is what will mark the difference between poor, good and excellent facilitators.

Four steps methodology

Active methodology starts at the observation and involves the apprentice in the immediate accomplishment of the task.

Stages:
1. Instructor says and does.
2. Participant says. Instructor does.
3. Participant says and does.
4. Participant does. Instructor checks.

Dynamical model of learning

The dynamical model of learning is based on the combination of adults' education (andragogy), playful activities, and constructive learning, so that effective changes can take place. It allows as well a good level of recollection in the participants, all of this in an environment of high participation and constant motivation.

Finally, handling four basic components of the learning: to think, to observe, and to make and to feel.

Those components are common to all of the active methodologies, whatever the fancy name we decide to use.

If a methodology lacks of some of these components, it cannot be considered an active methodology.

Ten basic skills for the facilitators

We see that OTEL relies on the individual, the human being. But although being a powerful tool by themselves, all of the OTEL activities need a catalyst, namely someone who accompanies the process from beginning to end. His name is Facilitator.

The learning processes developed thru active methodologies contemplate diverse skills which facilitate and propitiate the acquisition of new knowledge and its direct transference to the daily reality of the person, both personal and labor.

The suitable development of the whole learning process will depend on the attention given to the suitable combination and application of the skills and to its opportune inclusion in the formative program.

The Facilitator needs to dominate some specific skills.

A nostalgic picture. The OTEL pioneers in Spain. The first 6 facilitators. Back row: Alfonso, Philip, the author. Front row: Antonio, Xavi and Manuel.

1. Skills of "staging" (or framing)

They are the skills used at the beginning of every program in order to generate a few initial conditions of confidence and opening. During that phase of staging (or framing) the activities, the first approximation is realized by the participants:

- Greeting welcome.
- Discussion of expectations.
- Creation of shared attitudes which will be applied during the day.
- Setting of the methodology.
- Presentation of participants and facilitator.
- Definition of personal details: Duration, times of rest, etc.
- Activity "icebreaker" and rules for the day.

2. Skills of organization of groups
for the learning

The aim of these skills is to mobilize playfully, reflexively and/or actively the group, gaining its attention and concentrating the energy in benefit of the learning.

There are characterized for being activities of short duration, entertaining and that imply the free and spontaneous participation of the participants. Those can get confused with the timing of the day, as it does not always imply physical exercises.

There are also some "active pauses" (this is not a race or a contest). Individual and realized by the persons without the interaction with others, since they cannot interrupt the work of others.

The activities, nevertheless, are designed to be performed by the participants at the same time and space, independently of that it is a team or an individual activity. Everybody must feel involved one way or another.

3. Skills of reflection

The performed activities try to offer an experience which facilitates the learning and discovery which converges on situations in the real life of the participants.

Generally they are directed to propitiate close conceptualizations with regard to the subject in question or as a closing and reaffirmation of acquired knowledge.

4. Skills of Conceptualization

They imply that the application of the activities thru which a topic is approached for purposes of learning, having a theoretical and conceptual clear source and a definite scope.

The skills of conceptualization try to highlight the theoretical updated conceptions which endorse the object of the knowledge in order to construct, together with the participants of the learning, the new truths which from the analysis of the experience and from the support given by the facilitator, will shape the knowledge to be internalized and later applied by the participant and the facilitator himself.

They imply mental and rational processes of reading, analysis, interpretation, deciphering, transformation, exhibition and transference.

5. Skills of validation

In any process of training it becomes indispensable to verify and to assure that learning was understood by the group as well as by individuals.

It is an extremely productive moment of the process as the knowledge becomes reinforced by conclusions of the whole group.

6. Skills of Reinforcement

Complementary and with transverse application during the whole educational act, they try to verify that a concept or reflection has been learned or corroborated in a effective way, with the purpose of facilitating its learning.

Also, to reframe the discovery or appropriation of his own knowledge.

7. Skills of Closing

They try to gather and to consolidate the constructed knowledge and feelings demonstrated during the day. They are the activities which are done at the end of every educational intervention and include:

- Reflection about the experienced.
- Construction of individual commitments based on the generated knowledge.
- Evaluation: Of the performed activity as well as of the facilitator.
- Suggestions.

The closing can be partial, when the process still continues on the following day or in the posterior days; or when it finishes totally the educational intervention.

In any of the cases, closing is indispensable.

8. Adequate use of questions

The use of questions between the facilitator and the participants must be a constant during the whole educational process. For the specific case of the questions of the facilitator, these they must fulfill the following functions:

- To promote the active participation of the associates with regard to the topic.
- To stimulate the capacity of critical analysis and the creativity.

- To obtain information to know if the topic is remaining clear.

In order for the questions to be effective, they must be directed to the whole group, they must be allowed time enough for the elaboration of the answers, and finally they must be analyzed and given all the answers.

Many types of questions exist:
- Of direct information, (memory of recognition or evocation)
- Of focalization, (to reorganize information emphatically in the subject matter)
- Of opened end, (to generate variety of interpretations)
- Of evaluation, elaboration of judgments or criteria of value
- Of knowledge
- Of comprehension
- Of application
- Of analysis
- Of feedback

In the OTEL we also handle the following questions:

What did happen? It is realized at the end of the experience.

And it relates with? It tries to explore emotions, feelings demonstrated during the experience in order to relate them to the real life.

And now that continues? With the aim to generate links and relations between the lived experience and the labor or personal reality of the participants.

The most important thing, in any case, is to ask intelligent questions which propitiate the participation and the freedom of opinion.

Summarizing, have in mind those steps. These are the three questions which are to be asked.

1. What
2. So what

3. Now what
If we only ask the what, we are doing Outdoors adventure
If we ask the what and the so what, we have done Outdoor.
If we ask the three questions, we have achieved OTEL (outdoor or indoor)

9. Skills of empathy

Basically we are talking of active listening. The participants are out of their comfort zone, they are a very sensitive material and we are not in a sport contest.

10. Skills of non-verbal communication

Remember we are in the outdoors. If we want to convey tranquility, assurance, leadership, confidence, etc... we must rely on the non-verbal facet of communication.

Benefits in the use of skills of learning

Before going further, we must always have in mind the following. It is a sentence from one of our masters, Steve Webster: "Trust the process", always.

It works, so feel confident and always have in mind what are the eventual benefits for the participants, especially if you are facing some minor crisis (there are always some minor crisis during a OTEL session)

Some of the benefits of the application of OTEL as part of the active methodologies are:

They construct environments which promote and provoke the learning in suitable form.

Additionally they promote new behaviors, related with what was learned.

They bear in mind the cognitive processes associated with every cerebral hemisphere and facilitate the assimilation for persons with different styles of learning.

OTEL always works. The emotions are always waiting for you to blossom and lead to the acquisition of knowledge. The process is self-sustaining.

They involve all the related systems and integrate all the dimensions (physical, psychic, social, and spiritual).

They increase the learning and the efficiency of the participants, compared with other methodologies.

When the OTEL is used within a group, the confidence between the members increases by having been employed at uncommon tasks, tasks which demand the support and contribution of the whole group.

The accomplishment of dynamics in natural environments, offers the mind new and reinnovating actions applicable to different fields.

When having changed the environment, real conducts of the individual are highlighted and the curve of learning hastens, when as product of the above mentioned learning, they find new behavioral, more effective and productive options.

There are reinforced in a concrete way, inside a team, the responsibilities of the different persons in the consolidation of the processes of development and achievement of common aims.

Concrete results are obtained for the persons, for the teams, and for their organization or community.

Personal growth, integration, contribution of ideas, construction of new knowledge, enjoyment, change, respect for the others (experience of values), self-discovery, self-analysis, empowerment.

Dynamism in the learning.

Direct perception of attitudes, skills and knowledge.

Improvement in processes, improvement in motivation and sense of belonging.

"Learning by doing ", social and integral learning.

When having to design an exercise or a whole program, we must keep in mind all of the above. If one of them is missing, maybe we are not doing well.

Responsibility of the organization

And that brings us to a simple model; a model related to education is its higher significance.

The Educational Model defines.

To define the skills.

To have the aims clearly definite, to be coherent, to have a clear identification of needs, to do the follow-up, to respect.

Skills in the managing of unforeseen situations.

Coherence with the mission, aims and public of the organization.

Forecast of the logistics adapted in every moment.

To know the persons.

To develop individual plans of improvement.

To develop skills.

To plan adequately.

To respect the pace of learning of the participant.

To value the progress.

To realize processes of tutorship.

To realize follow-up and reinforcements.

To commit with the agreed.

Responsibility of the individual

But, first of all, let's not forget that the participant, as a first step, *does not want* to go out of his comfort zone nor to experience new things. The facilitator has to obtain:

- Attitude of change, enjoyment, aptitude to learn and forget.
- Commitment.
- To have goals of individual development.
- Disposition
- Put into practice the learned.
- Opening of mind and heart.
- To take part actively.
- Respect.
- To share his previous knowledge.
- Capacity of Self-evaluation.
- Humility, tolerance.
- Opening to the learning
- Disposition
- Discipline of self-study.
- Attitude of change.
- To transfer knowledge to the working place.
- To communicate knowledge.
- To support the competition.
- To commit to the agreed.

Another vital point: we see that we must move the people out of their comfort zone, in order for them to discover that the

OTEL can be useful for them, from a very selfish point of view, since this can turn out to be a great personal motivation.

If that process serves the company, much better. So, everybody wins.

Let's not forget one of the props of the OTEL and it is that it does not "attack" the analytical brain; it enters the emotions, though ultimately it is a question of developing cognitive structures, in order that those could be used when returning to work.

So, how does it work?

Methodology and strategy

Let's not lose of sight the aim, but let's have another look at some of the methodological foundations.

In any organization it is clear that to reach a major productivity, it is urgent to re think over the vision, the strategies, the leadership, the structure, the processes and the communications.

If we are going to compete and to grow in the modern world, we must assure the leadership, intelligence and collective commitment as some of our major guidelines for change.

In the mind of the competitors many ideas are being constantly adapted and improved. Even the technique can be bought by anyone who has the sufficient financial resources to do it.

What still has not been understood completely is that the real transformation is given in the thought and attitude of every human being and in the possibility of possessing agile and flexible processes handled by self guided cross functional teams orientated only towards a course: THE MARKET.

It is therefore urgent to accept that the success of an organization is the success of his people, orientating all of their talent, intelligence and ideas towards the improvement of the quality of the products and services.

We have to admit also that this responsibility cannot relapse into a few managers. We don't need heroes. The innovation has to be permanent and general and this is achieved by the collective leadership, though it sounds like an oxymoron.

The use of the talent and the creativity of all the collaborators is the only guarantee for survival and growth.

The new managerial success depends not only on the capacity fixing a vision and some strategies and criteria, but also on the aptitude for mobilizing the collaborators for the necessary implantation and later achievements.

Here it is when the system of training of OTEL receives importance.

Different investigations –and sheer common sense– have coincided in affirming that endless chats, tedious lecturers, flip charts full of statistical data, and long meetings with a never-ending flow of transparencies and slides have been the traditional ingredients of the managerial training.

Also we have the internal seminars where so much is invested and so little is harvested.

In general the collaborators return to work without having being "touched" and a high percentage ends up by thinking and doing the same thing as always and they forget what we tried to teach him during the seminar.

The companies facing this reality are looking for new forms of learning for their collaborators. The OTEL is one of them, and so far, the most productive without entering some more esoteric philosophies (namely NLP, Gestalt, transcendental meditation, new age introspection, and so on).

Here, no pun intended, as some of our colleagues have chosen that path, with some interesting results. Nevertheless, we think that all of those approaches can be suitable, in any case, for top managers or entrepreneurs who have already explored other ways.

We also think that, if those approaches work, they are concentrated on the personal self-development, assuming the posterior social skills development as a collateral benefit. Whatever; what interest us today is the development of skills more close to the daily experience in companies.

The participants of these experiences discover by themselves the concepts and new criteria which need to be reinforced; here being achieved a level of minimal recollection of 80 %. And that's measurable; it is not easy and requires of some special university probes, but some colleagues have been working on that specific issue, and their measurements and results are quite consistent.

The development of skills and the change in behaviors has to deal with exercises and real experiences, where the persons having faced challenges and complex situations, discover essential elements of the human behavior and the nature of the change, as well as the orientation to the productivity and competitiveness.

SOME KEY WORDS

AIM

Heaving the "aim". A 400 pounds iron logo.

Thru "OTEL" we try to reinforce the skills of leadership and teamwork, strengthening the strategic thinking and change in the organization as well as committing people with taking the necessary actions to consolidate the process of development of the Company towards a major competitiveness.

If we lose that aim, we have lost everything.

MODALITY

It combines processes for the identification, the learning and practice of the most relevant skills of leadership and teamwork, among others, although those are the basic ones.

Individual reflections are realized by the group helping them connecting with their own reality, and presentations are made to check the implicit concepts of the activities. Obviously, it is not enough to ask people whether they have understood and integrated. We must somehow ensure that this has been actually achieved.

EXPERIENCES

The absence of monotony and the playful aspect are the key for the great acceptation of this method. Emotional stimulation is vital in order to "reach" the inner person

The process of growth depends on its impact on the environment where it operates. To return to real world and to learn from it, it turns out to be highly satisfactory to develop skills of leadership and teamwork, and this way to increase the capacity of responding to the changeable requirements of the business.

In other words, once again, to be more efficient.

As we already said, for many people the reason of the success of this methodology takes its root in the application of the experimental education which handles four basic elements of learning: to think, to observe, to make and to feel.

So you must always wonder if, thru the OTEL experience you may be conducting, all of those four elements have been present.

It has the advantage of handling simultaneously both the emotive stuff and the cognitive stuff, which allows that the experiences should remain deeply ingrained and could be applied in posterior situations.

Let's see another definition:

It is possible to talk of "existential" instead of OTEL.

THE EXISTENTIAL LEARNING

The existential learning is "activated" when a person interferes in an activity of learning, analyzes the results of this learning and applies these results in his daily occupation. Actually, this process happens spontaneously and often in the daily life in each of us.

This is known as the "inductive" process. It has his roots in the observation and is opposite to the "deductive" process (based on the pre established truth).

The Course of Development of Skills of Leadership spins around this process, being based on the "Cycle of Learning" as a methodology of learning.

Let's have a look at this model, as it may help us developing an even more precise strategy for OTEL.

The cycle of existential learning in 4 steps

1. Experiencing

This first step is where the information is generated, and is associated frequently to the "nicest" step of the process, the "exercise", the graceful or happy thing.

Nevertheless, if the process ends with this first phase, there is no guarantee for a complete learning; the facilitator has not fulfilled his task.

In this step we might include the majority of the activities which help to the self-discovery and / or the interaction between persons.

In an OTEL program there are activities which allow to experiment:
- Planning
- Negotiation
- Case studies
- Skills between groups
- Simulation of roles
- Feedback
- Discovery of oneself
- Non verbal communication
- Solution of problems

The "inductive" learning means learning thru discovery, and can be done by means of permanent groups, groups "ad hoc", etc.

2. SHARING

Here the intention is to report and share the experience of every individual in terms of his "cognitive" learning (information) and "affective" learning (feelings towards me and other persons).

Some methods frequently used to share information in those courses are:

- Evaluation of productivity, satisfaction, confidence, leadership, exercise, communication, etc.
- You interview by pairs or subgroups
- Exercises of "guess who ", analysis of role exercised by different individual
- Opened and free discussion
- Interpreting

This step is the most critical of all, since it is a matter of systematical analysis of the experience which has been shared by all.

In this STEP it is important to stress that the "content" of the activity of learning is only a tool to assure that the "process" will be fulfilled.

3. EXTENDING

In this STEP it is necessary to give the great leap from the activity and its implications, from the controlled environment of this course, towards the reality of our daily life.

The key questions here are: What? Why? The participants must focus on situations of their personal and labor life, and extract information which will be useful for their daily occupation.

This step is the one of the Cycle of Existential Learning, and if the depth of the analysis were not the proper one, it would end in a rather superficial learning.

4. Applying

The final step of the Cycle of Existential Learning reflects the intention of the process in itself.

The key question in this step is now what? The facilitator will help the participants to apply the generalities towards real situations, but in terms of his future behavior in such situations.

Some Skills commonly used in those courses to achieve such an intention are:

- The teams, analyzing situations of the daily life
- Goals for short and medium term
- Personal and group commitments

It is more probable than the persons demonstrate this new behavior back at their normal environment if they have the opportunity of sharing their determination with others.

At that moment, and it might arise spontaneously, some system of support (friends, correspondence, periodic meetings) would be suitable to be launched, for the participants to feel some external support.

Conditions for an effective learning

The previously described Existential learning process only works for persons in situations of learning and requires certain requirements or previous conditions:

They must **want** *to learn*

The motivation for learning must come from the training directly; so we must analyze carefully the motives for being in the situation of learning. Now then, in real life, the majority of the people do not want to learn. Here the facilitator intervenes.

One must overcome his doubts and dreads

It is natural that people comes to situations of learning with certain doubts or dreads about their aptitude to learn, if they will be accepted by the group, if the experience will be agreeable and profitable, etc.

For such a reason the activity of learning must overcome these dreads as soon as possible, in order for the training to be productive. This change in the behavior, nevertheless, demands a basic effort from the facilitator, as it is his responsibility to help people achieving the change.

They learn by doing

The best way of learning any thing and to remember it for long periods of time is to use the information so rapidly and with so much frequency as possible. Again, the facilitator is vital in his labor of follow up.

The participant is sensitive to failure

The fear of failing must be replaced, in the activity of the learning, with the comprehension of what he learns more from of his mistakes than from his successes.

As the poet said: " the one who has not committed mistakes, has never achieved anything ", the failure, understood better, can turn into a springboard which stimulates us towards success.

We learn what has *personal meaning* for us.

If we can see the relation between what we experience in a situation of learning and its application in the real world, the learning will be much deeper and effective.

We must be emotionally prepared:

Often people come to a situation of learning with an armor of prejudices and convictions which they are not ready to break.

The result of this is the known" resistance to change " that eliminates any possibility of personal growth.

Likewise, a negative feeling would prevent the learning and individual growth, as well as the integration in the group.

The situation of learning must offer the opportunity to struggle with these obstacles and to promote a change in the personal behavior in the matter.

How can we tune that process of facilitation a little bit better?

Process of facilitation of the OTEL

Foundations

We name that way the basic and permanent criteria on which one leads a process of team making in the different circumstances it could happen.

Challenge for Options

It is the possibility of choosing in an individual way or in team the participation in one of the facilitated exercises.

It serves two basic purposes.

To avoid accidents and to trigger self-responsibility. As the person can so define his own limits and fully listen to his emotions.

To stimulate to the maximum the desire for challenge in relation with the value of self-overcoming and conquest.

The challenge for options has to be interpreted both by the facilitator and by the group for each one of the following parameters:

- Physical
- Emotional
- Spiritual
- Intellectual

If only one of them is not fulfilled, by the facilitator or by the participant, the option of learning must be postponed.

For such a motive, we see pertinent that this analysis is to be sequential in each of the moments of the experience (Before, During and Later).

So, in this step of the OTEL as well as in real and daily context of individual as application of constant improvement; we must condense the above-mentioned information into an instrument of compilation of information.

Contract of Added Value

It does relate to all of the aspects of profit as well as to the individual learning which is acquired thru having taken part in an OTEL program.

Generally the "contract" happens in the instant when expectations are leveled, when the aims of the group with relation to the experience are fulfilled, when the confrontation has been smoothed.

If strictly mandatory, the facilitator provokes some confrontation in the group, trying to change the behaviors which do not help the process.

This is done with supreme care:

He asks: why this attitude?

To outline the motive of what happened

The group has to elaborate its own tools of solution (to legitimize the way of using them).

One thinks about the fact, not about the personal attitude.

Relation Win-Win

It breaks the paradigm that during the exercise a loser has always to exist.

But here, nobody loses.

It is a vital point, as the human development is obtained from the potentials of the individual, not from his lacks and needs.

An Atmosphere of Property

It is the series of created mechanisms in order that the participant perceives a relaxed environment, so it allows a major degree of spontaneity, creation and cohesion of the group.

Respect for the intimacy of the Group

The facilitator stimulates the inner synergy of the group, not interfering with it, this being some intimate process.

Time Management

It is to consider from the beginning and during the course itself, the construction of the value of punctuality, stimulating the seriousness of the events, the dynamism of the group.

The personal limits

It emphasizes actions which demand to play at the limits of the allotted time.

These time limits are of free election and allow new knowledge, since especially in this case the participant becomes more conscious of the group.

The experience of the exercise

In the preparation of the exercise it is necessary to bear in mind:

- The name
- The levels of difficulty
- The intention or aim
- The needed materials
- The explanatory description and development
- The possible mechanisms of intervention and modification
- The minimal and maximum time
- Specification sheet of observation

It is considered of great importance, among the forms of motivation and interest which arise in the group and in each of the participants, the following thing:

The Fantasy: It is the fantasy life which raises the exercise and starts generating interest and restlessness of the participant towards the experience. That requires a great skill from the facilitator.

The staging: Decoration, the used materials and the correct link between them.

Application of the skills

The OTEL takes refuge in a technical design from which achievements of effective learning can be reached.

It refers to the access of the knowledge thru the experience (symbolic character of the learning), is articulated by the elaboration of concepts as Leadership, Communication, Teamwork, Planning, Taking of decisions, among others creating links in the sincere relation Experience, Previous Knowledge and Elaboration.

Conceptual integration like sharing space and socializing skills.

To begin relation with the daily reality.

Application and effective incorporations to the family, social or labor life.

Finding the practical value of the experience.

Ultimately these skills are the "Utilization of the exercises in an experience of learning for the own life".

The development of the training is realized as it is later detailed:

Name:

A label or identifying name for the technique reinforces not only its denomination simulative or fantastic, but it improves the limits in which participant influences the attitude of the group.

The name summarizes the essence of real or simulated experience.

GUIDE OF ELECTION OF ACTIVITIES:

Our experience with training of teams has demonstrated that the first exercise is chosen to strengthen teams, as well as it is designed to start fuelling the process once this one has been initiated.

Certainly, the election of an activity "by the book" does not constitute an unequivocal sign of success.

Multiple factors, from the "secret" roles of the participants, the not resolved expectations, up to reasons from the organization itself, are sufficient motives for thinking that the book is only a book, and the facilitator can adapt it. What's vital is that we must empathize with the group, and then decide whether or not we follow the initial script.

The guide presents a basic relation of the exercises, from minor to major difficulty. We propose 3 levels.

The activities of level 0 are simple, always; and the number of participants is not that relevant.

On the other hand, level 3 activities are of high difficulty, so it is for small groups instead. But first, the level of evolution.

LEVEL OF EVOLUTION

We name level of evolution the time the participants have already spent inside the organization, measured in years of interaction, so these can be the levels:

Basic group: Persons who have spent less than 1 year inside the organization.

Group of maturity: they are persons who have been interacting and sharing information and responsibilities, from 1 to 3 years inside the organization.

Group of high maturity: They are persons or members of the organization with a long relation of interaction and participation. More than three years inside the organization.

Size of the group

It is the number of persons who take part in the process of teamwork:

- Small: a group from 3 to 15 persons, handled by a facilitator.
- Medium: a group from 16 to 25 persons, still perfectly handled by a facilitator, though we recommend to rely on some assistant to support him at logistic level.
- Big: a group from 26 to 35 persons, which needs necessarily two parallel facilitators, and to divide the group in two.
- Giant: a group of more than 35 persons, up to 45 to 50 persons. Necessarily two facilitators and their assistant in logistics must handle it, and we must divide some activities in subgroups.
- Large programs: no limit. Though actually, our record is of 800 people together at the same time (1997, in the USA). Awesome logistics. You need to form pairs, one facilitator-one logistics. In total 40 professionals. Quite an experience... to be avoided if possible. Being so focused on logistics issues somehow hampers the outcome of the OTEL program.

LEVEL OF DIFFICULTY

It consists of the level of exigency and rigor of the activity for the members of the team.

The difficulty is not related only to the physical effort, but to the personal and emotional capacities of the group.

Basically, four types of difficulty exist. If we consider levels higher than 3, we are entering adventure or extreme outdoor. But that is not OTEL.

- Level 0: very low difficulty; they are exercises of sensitization towards the problematics of life and teamwork
- Level 1: Little difficulty, they are exercises of strengthening of the groups and potential teams.
- Level 2: Medium difficulty. They are exercises designed to facilitate the development of the teams.
- Level 3: High difficulty, they are exercises aiming at facilitating the redesign of the teams.

DYNAMICS AND LEVELS OF DIFFICULTY

Nevertheless, depending from the "dynamics" developed in the exercises, the skills acquire different degrees of actual difficulty (relation success/ frustration).

In general the exercises provoke sensations ranging from excitation to frustration, but its application obeys strict criteria of the dynamics of the group.

A level of difficulty must be calculated looking for a natural balance between the diagnoses we made of the group and the awaited achievements.

The Intention: We have already mentioned that the technical OTEL directs you to train groups in communicative skills, leadership and teamwork, because the technique aims at the above-mentioned intentions.

Nevertheless specific designs exist for three types of skills, so its intentions become very concrete.

The intentions of the OTEL skills must fit to the degree of training of the group, to the interest of development and certainly to the evolution the group demonstrates during the exercises.

Secondly, to encourage the playful component, as a way of learning and finally matching with the reflexive moments, the intentions and the evaluation.

The Materials

The experience is important for the participants, as they will manipulate the material, with its size, color, form and content.

They handle two types of material. Of permanent installation; and the transitory materials used solely for a specific exercise.

Basic material. Cartons, ropes, rubber bands, and generally any kind of "poor" material. Personally, we insist a lot on the "poorness" of the material, as we pretend people to feel they can achieve a lot with so little, just as in real life.

From our own experience, very often we can achieve outstanding results with some not so flashy −and expensive− activities.

Additional, safety materials are used in relation to the content of the exercise.

The Description

All of the OTEL exercises are orientated towards the accumulative learning of elements of personal training, by the explanation of its development.

TIME

The exercises are designed to be solved in a time of about 1 hour, but under the criterion of accumulating knowledge, the first exercises will be more flexible.

Additionally it has been considered to be the degree of achievement and / or frustration of an exercise not only the progress of the group, but also of the managing of the time.

THE FEEDBACK

The feedback understood as a construction is maybe one of the moments of major importance in the process, understanding that thru it the participant demonstrates and internalizes those aspects which hit his previous experience and which turns into aspects of improvement, transformation and changes of paradigm.

Dynamics of group and facilitation

In general the above-mentioned steps are, according to the model of Hickman

1. Birth (Naming)

Moment in which the persons get together to be mutually introduced, to chat casually (although nothing is really casual when talking about OTEL), to share interests, motivations and minimal organization interaction.

It is a transcendent moment providing that this one guarantees a starting point for the whole session.

Based on living together, they prepare for experiencing and learning thru the whole program OTEL.

Besides being the moment of mutual knowledge group/facilitator, we begin identifying roles, resistances and topics of principal attention in the participants.

Near Saarbruecken-Germany in the eighties. A motley crew of managers in the process of team making. The author, standing, third starting from the left, looking to the right.

2. STRENGTHENING (STORMING)

Here exists conscience of group and relationship.

Here, are made possible the evaluation of actions, the balances of consequences and their direct effects on the scope of collective achievements.

Possessing a strong and sure process of birth, the step of "strengthening" will appear inside the dynamics of structure as a moment adapted to provoke strong both individual and collective confrontations in the components of an OTEL exercise.

Here the conscience of the group favors the identification of accumulative knowledge.

With it, the group will acquire arguments of self-ingraining, self-overcoming and challenge for the following exercises.

The blockade of a group in this step will be a warning for reforming the birth in order to assure the incorporation of knowledge and its rapid progress, so that will indicate the need for accelerating the process and proposing exercises of major elaboration in team.

In this step, the most critical, we must be aware that normally, some serious conflicts may arise —and will arise— as this is the step of definition of roles, of confrontation, of evaluation and of confrontation.

And this is unavoidable. We must know we must go thru it, with the less possible damage, both for the group and the facilitator.

3. MATURITY (NORMING)

Now they have survived the storming step, they can analyze the reasons and consequences of their acts when dealing with resolution of problems, taking of decisions and leadership skills.

The group seeks to improve its methodology of action, finding importance in the exercise of the solidarity, the tolerance and the struggle for the common ideals.

The process of planning the development turns into the essence of the success, when the group exercises its responsibility in a methodical way.

For the facilitator, the fact that a group reaches this level implies the integration and correct development of the Outdoor exercises in the life of the group.

The group acquires the capacity of self-feeding and of proposing the alterations and adjustments which were previously induced by the facilitator.

Here the group has to be prepared to absorb the knowledge for its own experience and to find a logical application in real personal, family and labor life.

As the group evolves in an environment of constant interaction and necessary communication, the degree of commitment increases, preparing them for achievements of higher difficulty.

The whole process of aggrandizement of the group is fulfilled, and then the group must solve conflicts matching their levels of training.

The conflicts are an additive of "catharsis" in which the group exercises its attitude when having to overcome them.

For in the process: birth / strengthening / maturity, we talk about "crisis", when that forces the group to modify its performance and find equally collective solutions for the benefit for the group.

A crisis can be "natural" when it is the performance of the group who provokes it, or "induced" when it is an external element (facilitator) who manipulates it for educational intentions. He seeks the crisis to be pedagogic and didactic in benefit of the group.

4. Success (Performing)

Is the moment when a group self recognizes, self identifies with its reality and interests, assumes the crisis as a possibility of growth, and analyzes its skills.

Now it is self controlled by means of a constant analysis, and everyone starts perceiving the dynamics of "I am part of a Working Team" being this one the last goal of the facilitation of learning thru the OTEL.

The permanent role of the facilitation consists of creating both real and fictitious environments in order that the groups reach:

- Communication, feelings and convictions.
- Participation both in the action and in the taking of decisions.
- Levels of yield, or acceptable standards of performance.
- Penalties and stimuli / sensations.
- Sense of belonging.
- Definition of roles.
- When we come to this point, we have triumphed.

Learning by doing.
Some theoretical background

So we see that the OTEL is a powerful tool of transformation.

It allows us, in a simple, existential form, generating immediate enthusiasm, (performing activities of impact, outdoors), and acting on the persons, with the purpose of developing the emotional intelligence.

Personally, we don't like the word, as it is an oxymoron, but being fashionable enough, we can use it here.

So, as soon as we "move" the persons, we are developing their emotional intelligence, their own skills and their sensibilities.

That transports us to certain introspection in the psychological and emotional processes, generating very profitable and agreeable sensations.

This situation is completely necessary to achieve the wished growths and knowledge.

At the end, we understand that it is one of the few possible scenes (stages) for adults learning.

Let's remember Confucius, once again:

- "When I hear, I forget"
- "When I hear and see, I remember a bit"
- "When I hear, I see, I ask, I start understanding"
- "When I hear, I see, comment and practice I begin to acquire knowledge and skill"
- "When I teach, I dominate"

The OTEL has as background –though it is not the only one– Kolb's theories on the cycle of the learning and Honey and

Mumford 's on the styles of learning. These theories are object of debate, but many of the conclusions are pure common sense.

The cycle of learning is the base of all the OTEL programs.

The participants realize an activity, these activities can be outdoors or inside the classroom, and the activity provides a concrete experience to the participant.

After every activity we invite the participants to think about what happened or did not happen during the activity.

Towards the end of this reflection he devotes himself time enough to extract the knowledge of the activity, and to be able to apply it to the personal and professional life.

The conclusions of the activities combine with theoretical models to reinforce the learning.

Finally the participants take part in another activity in which they will have the chance of putting into practice what they have learned and of acquiring new experiences, that way returning to the first step of the cycle of learning.

Different persons learn of different forms. It is necessary to design the programs bearing in mind the different styles of learning in order for every participant to obtain the maximum from his experience. Four styles of learners are the most common in the cycle of learning:

Activists: They interfere to the maximum in the new experiences. Typically they act first and later they consider the consequences.

Thinkers: They like to give a step backwards to be able to observe what happens from several perspectives. They prefer thinking before acting.

Theoretical: From their observations they are capable of creating a logical theory. They prefer analyzing and synthesizing.

Pragmatic: They like to try new ideas, theories and skills to see if they work. They see the problems as a challenge.

Whatever the profile, anyway, during the activities we will notice that the persons "forget" certain behaviors they use at work and will show more natural behaviors; those difficult to see in daily work.

This promotes the development and the personal conscience.

When in an informal and relaxed environment in which these courses develop, the participants experiment with changes, new methods and attitudes without assuming the risks those experiments could represent back at workplace.

This foments the confidence and the support.

In these courses the learning is intense and rapid and helped by the new environment.

They leave behind those old behaviors and habits, allowing people to discover new and more original ways of learning.

The facilitators help to extract the behaviors, the actions and the attitudes which are relevant in the real world.

The participants are the ones who speak during the meetings reflections; the facilitator only guides the process.

This allows the participants to express their own point of view and to discover new aspects of their organization and of themselves.

The style of learning creates images and strong and lasting emotions which help to the personal discovery.

All the above-mentioned factors are combined to create the necessary impact and to drive the learning from mere theory up to real change, which is in essence the purpose of all the OTEL programs.

Practical OTEL

But in order for OTEL to be effective it is indispensable to take care up to the last detail before, during and after the exercise.

It is fundamental to know the values of the company, which skills we want to develop and then design a plan for measurement.

During the dynamics, the participants have to learn from the experience, relating their behavior during the exercise to their actual work. When designing an action plan of improvement and realizing a follow up in the company they complete the process.

In the OTEL the participants face challenges which need skills also necessary back at the workplace. This continues being vital; the OTEL has to have continuity in the labor or personal life.

The aim is that they learn from the experience and develop their skills. But in order for the process to be effective, it is indispensable to take care of all the details.

The program must be to tailor made and absolutely linked to the purposes, that is to say, to the strategy, aims, values and style of every company.

It is fundamental to know the company and the workers in their day after day living experience in order that they do not mislead you, claiming corporate values they do not feel in the company.

Some organizations realize an evaluation of the professionals who are going to take part in the program.

Every candidate is self-evaluated and asks several collaborators for a feedback. The aim is that they discover which aspects they can improve

The exercises have to be designed depending on the characteristics of the professionals who are going to perform them.

Those vary depending on the age on the participants and on the style of the company. They are not the same for a conservative company and for a more aggressive one.

Anyway, the simpler the activity, the more opportunities to think about the exercise.

"It is more worth moving water cans than doing a rappel descent".

We also think that sometimes it is of great interest generating some conflict between the members of the group, to observe their reactions.

The playful part of the exercises serves for the participants to feel comfortable and be themselves, to later relate the activities to work.

Besides, the fact that they all are in sports footwear and without tie helps to democratize the training. Everybody is "equal".

Here, an important advice: Be very careful of not giving the sessions a "Yankee" touch. In Spain, and generally in Western Europe countries, we have a sense of the ridicule more developed than in Anglo Saxon cultures.

Equally, it is not necessary to forget that the curve of learning and involvement is not the same for every human being, so we must respect it.

And that is difficult! But this is what allows us to distinguish between a good OTEL facilitator and a mere sports entertainer.

After the activity, it is the moment to analyze the exercises (the step of debriefing), to see the different attitudes and to relate them to their daily work.

But they are the own professionals those who have to analyze what has happened and to comment what aspects could have been better developed.

The facilitator, besides forming them in the exercise in question, acts as a trainer and helps the participants extracting conclusions and developing the specific skill there are experiencing at that moment.

In the OTEL programs, the professionals later face a second similar exercise, though always slightly different from the former; (in order that they always have to move out of their comfort zone, and therefore always continue experiencing new things, so they put into practice the acquired knowledge.

This serves them as a practice and validation of what they have learned. So they can see how they have improved using the taught methodology. But, never repeating the exact activity, to avoid the exercise becoming a mere playful game.

OTEL uses games, but is not a game. It is a session of work and analysis, albeit entertaining and exciting.

In spite of the fact that the persons and their conducts are analyzed, the OTEL is used for forming the professionals, not for evaluating them.

Besides, we recommend that the groups should not be of more than fifteen persons, because the capacity of analysis is minor. Equally, a too small group (less than 10 persons) cannot work.

Action Plan

As soon as the dynamics has been analyzed, it is indispensable to design an action plan, which can be individual or as a group.

This one must be as concrete as possible and must include objectives of improvement, actions which must be implemented, the expected deadline and the person in charge who will guarantee its fulfillment.

Later, it is indispensable to realize a follow up of what has been obtained and the encountered difficulties or possible blockades.

The day after is the most difficult. Many professionals leave the session with something learned but often coherence is absent back at the workplace.

In many OTEL projects, we have seen how after the action, the "fire" abates after a few weeks.

So beware, never forget that the aim of this technique is to promote the development of skills and indispensable attitudes in the daily work. (It should not remain as a merely "Day of the tortilla"!).

The OTEL is a technique which offers the companies to form his personnel "outdoors" and to promote the learning thru the direct experience in a distended environment.

The OTEL is an alternative (though it does not replace it in all circumstances) to the classic training, based fundamentally on the oral methodology (courses, presentations, seminars, etc.), and he looks for reinforcing the skills of the personnel thru the analysis of conducts, attitudes and relations between the team members.

The programs of OTEL are specially designed for small teams of professionals: they combine outdoor activities with reflection meetings which promote, thru the practice and the experience, the change in the way of thinking and acting of the participants, affecting them in those aspects it is necessary to reinforce (leadership, taking of decisions, personal development, etc.).

And what are the activities which are going to allow us to obtain all that?

Example

The activities generally develop in a natural environment and thru teams of work. The activities are orientated to face

Bow shooting can be used as an energizer, and as a tool for developing concentration. We make three different teams, but we do not frame it as a sports competition. The author in the center, wearing a cap and giving advice.

different "challenges". When we talk about challenges, we do not talk about competition.

Some of the most common activities are the following ones:

The climbing wall seeks to develop the support between colleagues, overcoming the fear of highs, used as an excuse. This allows us to practice the moving out of the comfort zone, as a route for personal discovery and learning.

Extinction of fires: coordination is vital if we want to extinguish the fire.

Constructing a raft, a cabin, and a bridge: the aim is to foment the work in team and the confidence between colleagues.

Night orientation: the teams must orientate during the night, for example in a forest. This practice tries to develop the taking of decisions, the communication between the persons and specially to foment the leadership towards the group.

But let's not forget that the activities are a way, not an end.

The men who help us.

A program of OTEL goes beyond offering outdoor courses and exercises. There is something fundamental behind these activities, and it is the group of facilitators who helps all the participants to interpret the results of the different exercises about what is happening.

The aim is clear: the employee must assume a commitment of improvement with his company. To obtain it, the companies or schools of training have to detect beforehand which are the needs of every organization. It is here where the role of the Person in charge of Human Resources is key.

Once one has interviewed all the members of the team and there has been realized a diagnosis of the needs of the company, a plan of action is designed with all the necessary tools and dynamics.

Later, there comes the step of learning; where the personnel and managers are busy during 2 or 3 days, challenging the elements of the nature: land, water and air, out of their habitual scenes.

After passing the exercises, we help them detecting the strong and weak points derived from the behaviors of the team and linking these attitudes to the habitual conducts at work.

Finally, we elaborate an action plan, which includes the different aspects to be improved and are applicable to the company.

DEVELOPMENT OF CAPACITIES

The programs of OTEL are never standardized —or at least they should not be— since they come determined by the needs of the clients. In spite of this, the aims those practices are seeking for are orientated basically to the promotion and evaluation of the performance of the personnel and in fomenting the following professional and personal capacities:
- To foment the communication between all of the members of a company.
- To control the job stress and to improve the capacity of reaction in front of any situation of pressure.
- To increase the confidence between colleagues.
- To promote teamwork to achieve cooperation between the members of the company.
- To promote the taking of decisions, the leadership and the aptitude to delegate responsibilities.

- To motivate the personnel in the commitments of daily work.

The assimilation of the concepts thru this type of training aims at improving the attitudes of the professionals thru attractive activities which have a direct effect on the internal cohesion of the organizations.

AN EXAMPLE

In this example of a course of three days (we think that three days is the maximum admissible duration, not to enter into activities of pure adventure, which are another thing altogether), let's return again to the why of the OTEL.

To do OTEL, with physical exercises and activities of group, means first, to decide to learn thru experience, to undertake and to be responsible for the own process of growth.

Also it means to identify aims for the team, and at the same time, personal plans of development designed by each one and discussed with the group.

It supposes considering every activity not as an entertaining and nice "exercise" but as a metaphor of what happens in the company, of the dynamics of interpersonal relation which are to be developed, of the taking of decisions and of the daily situations of assumption of risks which take place, and of the different types of leadership that may exist.

Often this means accepting personal challenges and deciding at every moment about the next move.

It also means valuing the group, the different roles for the different activities and the diverse but equally important contributions the others bring in every situation.

In this company we use as example, the human resources' department considers necessary to live this experience together.

It was decided that "to make team" would be the fundamental premise, with the participation of all, with no discrimination because of roles and responsibilities, all of them consciously being part of the same structure.

In the step of planning were identified the most specific areas of improvement, which were used later to orientate the activities as "aims of the group" during the three days of the program.

These aims are widely linked to the nature of the work developed today within Human Resources, constructed by processes characterized by long period, high risk, continuous taking of decisions, and use of internal and external resources to the company.

It was necessary to focus the attention of everybody towards the aptitude to confront risks and to take decisions, towards self-confidence and group confidence, towards the knowledge of the different leadership styles, towards the disposition for moving out of the comfort zone, towards the quality of the communication and the need to integrate internal and external skills.

The experience

It turns out to be very exciting being tied on a cable of steel, suspended at more than 15 meters of height, hand in hand with the colleagues, and finding the inner strength for continuing forward, in spite of the fear, thanks to the stimulus of the rest of the group.

As they are tied together, they have to climb simultaneously. There is no other alternative. They are responsible for the success of the pair, not only for the individual one, individual success which, by the way, cannot be attained for obvious reasons.

Many times, the improvement of the self esteem coincides with the improvement of the esteem of the group, so this allows us to overcome in a natural way, the self imposed limits, without being forced to do it.

Finally, it turns out to be exhilarating to be gathered at the foot of a climbing wall, which represents our obstacles, and to climb it thanks to the support of the others, and discovering that we can only go as high as the weakest link of our human chain. So, as we are tied, the only solution is to collaborate. The metaphor is undisputable.

Identified the obstacles which prevent us from reaching the objective, we propose to find the best strategy to overcome them, developing a strong feeling of participation and belonging to the group.

Each of these activities is highly didactic, because they are followed by moments of individual reflection shared with the group (debriefing), and these suggestions are used to improve or to reinforce the conduct of each one (feedback).

The debriefing is without any doubt the section of more difficulty but also the most constructive –in fact it is the vital part–, permitting us to translate what we experiment during the physical activities, to express personal emotions, to analyze the reason of our success or failure in the tasks, and to be able to transfer it to the workplace.

This way the "exercises" turn into metaphors on the organization we are part of, and help us identifying strengths and areas of improvement. Then, everybody commits himself with assuming responsibilities thru a Personal Action Plan.

But this is not the end, because, what happens next?

Later, it is necessary to foresee and organize a day of follow up a few months later, when everyone will expose the progresses realized in his personal plan of development.

It is also always necessary to insist that this experience is not limited to the days of the OTEL activity, but is part of an Action Plan for Human Resources Department. Aimed at developing processes and systems of taking of decisions, evaluations of skill, managerial conducts, individual training and communication.

With regard to the communication especially, the Plan has to prosper later with suggestions and offers which should be born out of a group expressly organized during the last session of OTEL.

The challenge now is to support the spirit and the teamwork that always characterizes OTEL sessions.

And this part is not the easiest, because often we have seen experiences in which one neglects the follow up, beginning to lose the acquired during the OTEL days.

Let's remember that it is possible to produce even rejection if this follow up is not done.

APPLICATION TO LEADERSHIP

Now, with these principles in mind, let's enlarge the scope of the OTEL. If what we want is to develop guidelines of leadership, it is possible, though it is only a small part of the possibilities.

So let's have a look from the point of view of the leader, or the potential leader.

By means of the challenging and playful experiences whether indoor, or outdoor, these programs assure the transmission of the specific and necessary knowledge assuring the development and training of the pertinent skills and the acquisition of attitudes orientated to the achievement and the performance in all of our activities.

Today it is imperative to reach high levels of skills and quality in all our activities. For it is necessary to train all our potential and to develop strategies orientated to the achievement. We must acquire and develop four kinds of skills:

1. Diagnosis of Personal skills and Organization.
2. Technical and Specific knowledge.
3. Personal and Social skills.
4. Attitudes orientated to achievement.

These formative programs demand a high commitment for action.

OTEL methodology for the leader

The formative actions which we can tackle to acquire skills range from verbal lecturing of some technical knowledge (little efficiency, since you just listen), to the experience of direct experiences (great efficiency, better acquisition).

We all have verified this principle in the training: "it is learned basically from the experience".

The direct experiences are much more effective for our progress than the verbal theoretical symbology

These programs have a major impact than other methodologies, and a better ratio investment / result obtained.

What is leadership? Can we think of some basic key words?

- The leadership is an invisible thread
- As mysterious as powerful, which drags and joins.
- It is a catalyst which creates unit from disorder.
- Nevertheless, it defies any definition.
- No combination of talents guarantees it.
- No process of training will be able to create if the initial spark does not exist.
- The qualities of the leader are universal.
- They are qualities which suggest paradoxes more than a scheme.

But when they find these qualities, the leadership does make things happen.

The most precious and intangible quality of leadership is the confidence. The confidence they are able to convey.

That confidence will act in the best interest of his followers, without sacrificing the rights of the individual.

The imperative of the leadership is:

"A sense of the correct thing and the opportune thing":

To know when to advance and when to do a pause.

When to criticize and when to praise and how to encourage the others to stand out.

From the reserves of energy and optimism of the leader, the followers extract his own strengths, from his determination and self-confidence, they find inspiration.

In the highest sense, the leadership is integrity; aimed at conscience, commitment and example.

The integrity recognizes external obligations, but he attends to the serene voice of the interior more than to the exterior clamor.

The only way of exploring the development of these skills is experiencing.

If we are not naturally gifted, the only way of developing our leadership skills is to experiment, not just intellectually understanding what it is all about, but practicing in an OTEL environment.

How to practically
develop a program

What steps do facilitators consider before initiating the activities themselves?

Valuing

In this first step information is gathered. We fill some forms, thru written or oral interviews, surveys of attitude, etc.

Identifying what the organization wishes to achieve and who they are, will make possible to predict the type of activities which will be more appropriated.
- Some questions to be formulated
- Who is the organization?
- Which are its interests?
- Do workers want to take part in this type of activities?
- Has the leader the same goals as the participants?
- How many participants will enter the program?
- Where will the program take place?
- Etc...

Planning

It allows us selecting the tools that will be used, using the details gathered during the valuation as a reference. We decide the design of the activities.

Having gathered the necessary information from the interested parties meant to be involved in the activities we will be able to answer the following questions:

What activities will be necessary to achieve the wished aim?

What sequence of activities will produce good results?

What Skills will be necessary to break the ice, offering the necessary confidence?

How much time the activities will last?

How to handle the resistance of the groups?

What personnel will I have to rely on to succeed with he program?

PREPARING

Preparing OTEL activity

It allows putting in order all the elements of the step of planning. It implies gathering all the materials that will be needed; coordinating with the colleagues, making sure that they all should understand the plan; and finally checking the site, determining if the selected activity is the most appropriate.

What steps do facilitators consider during and after the OTEL activities?

The cycle of the activities of the OTEL is based on the existential learning process; the one which consists of 5 clearly definite stages, based on the inductive process:

EXPERIENCING

Here the information is generated. It develops the inductive learning, that is, learning by doing and discovering, thru groups, triads, etc.

SHARING

Here we share the experience of every individual in terms of his learning intra and interpersonal (affectively) and cognitive.

Open and free discussion

Exercises and games like " guess who ", analyzing the roles exercised by each of the participants.

Evaluation of the productivity, satisfaction, leadership, communication, etc.

We interview by pairs or by subgroups.

INTERPRETING

It is considered to be the most critical step of all. When having been carried out a systematical analysis of the shared experience, having analyzed what really happened inside the group, the individual and collective behavior and the effect on the participants.

EXTENDING

The participants will analyze and ask themselves: So What, Now What?

Focusing on their personal and labor life, similar to the realized activities, extracting information which will be useful for their daily occupation.

This one is the step which gives him or her sense or this program. If not being treated adequately and with the depth it requires, it would turn out to be a superficial learning.

APPLYING

Here the intention is reflected in itself. The key question is now what?

The facilitator will help the participants to apply the learned to real situations, in terms of his future behavior.

The Skills most used to achieve this intention are:

The groups, analyzing situations of the daily life.

Commitments both at personal and team level.

Identification of goals at short and medium term.

If we bear in mind the previously exposed, the OTEL program will work.

If we keep the Decalogue in mind, we will not lose contact with the initial aim.

Let's finish then the theoretical part with some reflections, widening the scope of all the principles we have been talking about.

Part 3
Theoretical bases for OTEL

TRAINING AND DEVELOPMENT
OF COGNITIVE STRUCTURES

So let's try to enter some more profound aspects, in order to understand what really happens when using those methodologies.

These concepts are a little bit arid but they deserve us to devote some time to think over them.

Learning is a process of development of effective structures. It identifies the knowing, defined as "comprehension of the meaning". When a hesitation or doubt exists in the learning, that means it has not been fully understood.

The training and development of the cognitive structure depends on the way a person perceives the psychological aspects of the personal, physical and social world.

The motivations depend on the "cognitive structure"; and the change of motivation implies a change of cognitive structure. By means of the learning are produced the changes of internal comprehension of the situation and his meaning.

The changes which take place in the cognitive structure come for the change in the same structure and for the strength that they have in "here and now" the needs, motivations, desires, tensions, aspirations, etc.

Here we concentrate on the orientation of the learning which supposes the genesis of new internalized concepts, new mental structures, new attitudes... with that the participant could analyze and solve the problems.

The new structures and attitudes developed by the assimilation, reflection and self-absorption, allow us to value and to dig a little bit deeper into the different vital situations where we have to choose a personal option.

A reflexive process exists, so, as it is a question of incorporation conscious and responsible for the facts, concepts, situations, and experiences, and that it implies accepting the learning from the perspective of the participant and related to specific areas.

Therefore, it is a question of learning about how to develop the critical attitude and the capacity of the taking of decisions. These two characteristics define the process of "learning to learn".

Why do we present it that way? For a simple reason, at least from our point of view: as learning is a conscious act –although not always, we admit it– and should we say, is an actual skill, therefore it can be practiced in order to improve it, just as any other skill.

Learning has not a lot to do with repetitive learning, although thru repetitive learning, we can learn something, but the yield factor is quite poor.

Inside our conception, it is important to clarify first the concept of cognitive structure. Some colleagues define it as "hypothetical constructions, that is, supposedly hypothetical entities which must explain the whole, connecting similarities and coincidences of certain manners of behavior". Well, whatever...

We use the concept in order to designate the knowledge of a certain topic and its clear and stable organization. For that purpose we use the cognitive structures, and it is in connection with the type of knowledge, its extent and its degree of organization.

We support that the cognitive structure of a person is the factor which conditions the significance of the new learning material and its acquisition and retention. That's our real concern.

The new ideas can be learned and retained only if they relate to some already available concepts or propositions, those providing the conceptual "anchors" or "hooks".

The involution of the cognitive structure of the participant facilitates the acquisition and retention of the new knowledge.

If the new material enters a strong conflict with the cognitive existing structure or if it does not connect with it, the information cannot be incorporated nor retained, although it can be –at least for a while– memorized.

The participant must think actively about the new material, thinking about the links and similarities, and reconciling differences or discrepancies with the existing information.

This, briefly, and in an OTEL situation, tells us that: Whether we receive some reward –whatever the reward, analytical or emotional– appealing to the cognitive structures of the participants, or any program will fail.

This has to do with the mental schemes which shape our structure of learning, of skills (aptitude), but also of Attitude.

Although the word "learning attitude" sounds as an oximoron, since attitudes cannot be learned, it is possible to experience them.

Effective learning and repetitive learning

OTEL Learning is effective learning, in a sense that we should never repeat an already performed exercise. That's one of the main differences between effective learning and repetitive learning.

On having analyzed the school reality, we realized that it was predominating a repetitive learning, characterized by the acquisition of the knowledge thru a few repetitive procedures.

We are not sure –to put it mildly– that this the proper way of developing the human being and his acquisition of learnings.

The alternative is when the participant acquires the knowledge by himself, that is, when he re-discovers it, without giving him a previous learning scheme organization.

Learning thru discovery is the alternative to repetitive learning.

For us, the distinction between repetitive learning and effective learning is more important, as it relies on more coherent criteria of contraposition.

The repetitive learning takes place when "the task of learning consists of pure arbitrary associations" (numbers, lists, associate couples, etc.).

In the association of the concepts there is no substantial relation and no logical meaning.

In the repetitive learning, the new information does not associate with the existing concepts in the cognitive structure and, therefore has a minimal or even a non-existent interaction between the recently acquired information and the already stored information.

The participant does not have any intention of associating the new knowledge with the structure of concepts which he already possesses in his cognitive structure. A mechanical memorization takes place, thru repetitive information, facts or concepts.

The effective learning, on the contrary, takes place when we establish relations between the new concepts or new information and the concepts and existing knowledge already ingrained in the participant, or with some previous experience.

There is effective learning when the new information can relate, in a not arbitrary and substantial way (not word by word) with what the participant already knows.

Hereby, the participant constructs his own knowledge and, besides, he is interested and determined to learn.

Summarizing, the differences between both types of learning are the following ones:

In the effective learning, the new information relates, on a substantial, not arbitrary form, to the cognitive structure of the participant. There is a premeditation of relating the new knowledge to the one already existing in the cognitive structure.

It relates to the experience, facts or objects. There is an affective implication on having established this relation, on having demonstrated a positive disposition prior to the learning.

In the repetitive learning, the incorporation of the new knowledge takes place in an arbitrary form. There is no intention of integrating them in the cognitive structure. It does not relate to the experience, facts or objects.

There is no affective implication in the above-mentioned relation for not having showed a positive disposition before the learning.

Nevertheless, we do not conceive these two classes of learning as radically opposed, but presenting them as a continuous one.

The effective learning is more effective than the repetitive, fundamentally because it affects the three principal phases:

1. Acquisition
2. Retention
3. Recovery

The realized exercises confirm that the effective approach of a potentially effective material makes the acquisition easier and more rapid than in the case of a repetitive approach.

The effective acquisition is easier because fundamentally it implies the utilization of structures and previously acquired elements; what we call "hooking" or "anchoring" with regard to the new material, for similarity and contrast. Also, after an OTEL activity, the emotions felt are the hook for anchoring the learning in posterior real life.

It is retained more easily during a longer period.

When does effective learning take place?

With stripes of cardboard, staples and little more, a competition between three teams, in order to construct the sturdiest little tower. This activity is used for stretching bonds, and strengthening the sense of belonging to "my" team.

The fundamental of the effective learning as a process consists of the fact that the thoughts, expressed symbolically, connect with the already existing knowledge in the subject. This process, so, is an active and personal process.

It is an active one, because it depends on the deliberate assimilation of the task of learning from the participant.

It is personal, because the meaning of the whole task of learning depends on the cognitive resources which every participant uses.

The key of the effective learning is in relating the new material to the already existing ideas in the cognitive structure of the participant. Consequently, the efficiency of this learning is depending on his inner meaning, not on repetitive learning skills.

For it, the basic requirements are:

That the material is potentially effective, that is to say that it allows establishing a substantial relation with knowledge and already existing ideas.

The trend of the participant towards effective learning, that is to say a disposition in the participant who indicates interest to devote himself to a learning which tries to give a sense to what he learns. Caution: remember that this is not a natural trend for us human being; it demands us to move out of our comfort zone.

A POTENTIALLY EFFECTIVE MATERIAL

When is material potentially effective?

The potential significance means that the material of learning can be put in connection. In a not arbitrary or superficial way, consistent with the cognitive structure of a certain individual.

In general, we can say that the new material must be "capable of giving room to the construction of meanings".

The new material must allow a meaningful relation (not arbitrary) and substantial with the knowledge and ideas of the participant.

By "substantial relation" there it is understood that this relation is established by some specifically relevant aspect of the cognitive structure of the participant, as an image, an already effective symbol, a concept or a proposition.

It is a therefore a matter of the relation which is established by the sense and meaning of the previous ideas. The effective relations can express normally in diverse ways and its establishment is easier when one resorts to alternative formulations.

This potential "effectiveness" of the material depends on the logical meaning, that is to say, that the content or material possesses an internal, organized structure, in such a way that its fundamental parts have a meaning in itself and are related between them in a not arbitrary way.

This potential logical effectiveness not only depends on the internal structure of the content, but also on the way it is presented to the participant.

Here appears the critical figure of the OTEL facilitator, as it is his responsibility to ensure that the logic is respected.

AN ATTITUDE AND ITS PSYCHOLOGICAL EFFECTIVENESS

Besides the logical effectiveness, the material or content of learning of potential psychological effectiveness needs elements which could mean something for the participant and could lead him into taking the meaningful decision of relating it to his own knowledge.

This explains the importance of the ideas or previous knowledge of the participant in the process of effective learning.

The psychological effectiveness supposes, so, the availability of relevant contents in cognitive structures of different participants, that is to say, that the participant has in his cognitive structure the design to which he could relate the new material.

And it will be an important responsibility for the facilitator to ensure this is correct. Otherwise, we are pouring information into a bottomless pit.

So, besides the potential effectiveness, logical and psychological, of the material, another basic condition is needed: a favorable attitude of the participant to learn effectively, that is to say, an intention of giving sense to what it is learned and of relating, not arbitrary, the new material of learning to his knowledge acquired before and to the already constructed meanings.

Here, once again, do not forget how difficult it is to move out of the comfort zone. It is not a natural impulse, so we must create the conditions for that move.

Summarizing, the effective learning presupposes three conditions in order to work.

The new materials or information to be learnt must be potentially effective, in order to being able to be related to the relevant ideas the participant possesses.

The cognitive previous structure of the participant must possess the necessary relevant ideas in order that they can relate to the new knowledge.

The participant must have effective disposition towards the learning, which demands an active attitude. If not, we must, previously to any activity, start with some warm-up activities, in order to generate a minimum of enthusiasm or mere curiosity towards what we are going to experience during our OTEL session.

Types of learning

We are seeing that something as "natural" as learning may not be that easy, and as well as other topics or techniques, there are several theories and points of view.

There are three basic types of effective learning depending on the increasing degree of complexity: learning of representations, learning of concepts and learning proposition.

1. Learning of representation

It consists "of being done by the meaning of sole symbols (generally words) or by what those represent".

It is a question of learning what the isolated words or the symbols mean.

It means learning the particular symbols which represent or are effectively equivalent to the specific modals.

This type of learning links itself with the acquisition of the vocabulary. In the learning process of representations it is necessary to distinguish two aspects:

- The learning before the concepts.
- After the training of concepts.

In the first one, the words represent objects or events. The word is equal to the concrete and specific image of what such modals mean.

We won't enter here any debate, as this is not our domain of expertise, but linguists well know that depending on the language, the process of associating words and concepts differ from one language from another. Those who are fluent in German know how much that language for instance appeals to literal descriptions, when most of the indo European languages have a more symbolic way of constructing and associating words and concepts.

But, as the poet would say, that's a different story.

What's significant for us is that the adult –or the child– when he develops, learns new vocabulary to represent concepts.

2. LEARNING OF CONCEPTS

It is the second type of effective learning. This concept is defined as "objects, events, situations or properties which possess attributes of common criterion and which are designated by means of some symbol or sign".

The concepts also represent symbols and individual words, but there is a major degree of abstraction depending on a few common attributes of criterion. They arise, so, from relating certain objects, events, etc. with common attributes, to all of them.

We assume two forms for the learning concept: one, training of concepts from the concrete experiences, similar to the learning representation, and, second, the consistent assimilation of concepts in relating the new concepts to the already existing ones in the participant forming conceptual structures.

3. LEARNING OF PROPOSITIONS

It consists of "catching the meaning of new ideas expressed in the shape of propositions", that is to say, expressed in a phrase or sentence which contains several concepts.

Some specialists indicate that "the propositions are two or more concepts tied in a semantic unit... Using a rather coarse metaphor, the propositions are the molecules with which the meaning is constructed and the concepts are the atoms of the meaning. Whatever, what is important for us, from an OTEL point of view, is the importance of logic between experiences, concepts, analysis and integration?"

Put in other words, an OTEL session must be very cautious about the logical flow of activities, in order to avoid the repetitive learning (negative) effect, where things don't flow out naturally from the participant.

This type of learning can be done, combining or relating individual words between them, each one with a different modal, and combining them in such a way that the result (the proposition) is more than the sum of the meanings of the individual concepts.

Logically, in both previous types of learning it is a matter of representations or unitary concepts, whereas in the learning proposition intervene several concepts which relate to themselves and to the cognitive structure of the participant to produce a new consolidated meaning.

All of this can sound quite obscure, to put it mildly. Being practical, what we can say is that, on having implied relation of concepts, the acquisition of the propositions can be done only thru assimilation.

THE LEARNING LIKE PROCESS OF COMPREHENSION AND ASSIMILATION

When we talk about what the participants "understand", we are saying that they should try to give shape to the representations and the cognitive schemes which are formed in their minds.

It is a question, so, of an active, consistent assimilation in grasping or acquiring the concepts involved in the learning process, which go from the mere sensory characteristics up to the most abstract characteristics.

To facilitate the comprehension and the assimilation, every person has his strategies, but it is possible to affirm that the familiarization with the material has a major positive impact; better anyway than if dealing with unknown material. Using these familiar materials to establish relations, classifications, categories, schemes, facilitates a more effective learning.

Once again, we insist on the utilization of anchors or hooks, in order to ensure that the acquired learnings are actually acquired and remain forever, being now part of the "developed" participant.

Think of the implications: if we manage to achieve that, we have touched the deepest nerve and reached the core of the person; we have modified the Attitude.

We have achieved the most difficult part. We have helped people integrating (assimilating) concepts.

THE ASSIMILATION OF MEANINGS
AND ITS MODALITIES

The theory of the assimilation is the central point of our approach on effective learning, in such a way that most of this learning consists of the assimilation of new information.

It explains the above-mentioned theory saying that the new information is linked to the relevant and preexisting aspects in the cognitive structure, and in the process where are modified the recently acquired information and the preexisting structure.

Some would say: we can learn just what we can learn. Well, whatever … So the question could be: How can I know how much I can learn, both in terms of quantity (the railway timetables from London to Manchester) and of quality (the first law of thermodynamics, which explains how trains work).

Obviously, there is no way –no actually known way– of probing those limits. This statement can sound somehow heretic, but were it to be true, we would be able to, prior to any learning session, measure the limits of the potential comprehension ability of our participants, and therefore precisely tune both message and vector of the learning concepts.

Presently, we cannot give a global and effective response to this utopia.

The acquisition of new information depends in high degree of the pertinent ideas which already exist in the cognitive structure; and the effective learning of the human beings happens thru an interaction between the new information and the pertinent ideas which exist in the cognitive structure.

The good news –human being a non deterministic entity– is that fortunately, we haven't fathomed yet that deep into the human brain, so we don't know the actual limits, or simply put, the boundaries which prevent us from acquiring those knowledges.

The process of interaction between the material newly learned and the existing concepts constitutes the nucleus of the theory of the assimilation.

The process of assimilation works by means of three forms or different modalities:

1. Subordinated learning

The new idea or concept is hierarchically subordinated to an already existing one. It takes place when the new ideas relate to relevant ideas of major level of abstraction, generality and inclusiveness.

There is generated a progressive differentiation of the existing concepts in several levels of abstraction.

In the instruction process, the progressive differentiation consists of departing from the most general ideas to come down to the most concrete, splitting progressively the concepts into subconcepts.

2. Learning supraordinated

The process is inverse to the subordinate or process of progressive differentiation, where the relevant concepts existing in the cognitive structure are of a minor degree of abstraction, generality and inclusiveness than the new ones to be learnt.

With the acquired information, the already existing concepts are reorganized and acquire new meaning.

When differences, comparisons and similarities are looked for between the concepts, this conceptual reconciliation is facilitated.

When a concept connects well with another more general concept, it possesses a cognitive agreement or an integration and reconciliation.

And last, there is obtained a cognitive dissonance, when two concepts contradictory appear not adequately integrated.

3. Combinatorial learning

It consists of a relation, of a general form, of new concepts with the already existing cognitive structure, but without being produced the incorporation.

It relies on the search for common elements between the ideas, but without establishing a relation of supra or subordination.

We think that the cognitive structure is organized hierarchically with regard to the level of abstraction, generality and inclusiveness of the ideas or concepts.

In the subordinated learning and supraordinated learning a hierarchic relation exists, whereas it does not take place in the combinatorial learning.

THE COMPREHENSION OF MEANINGS

The effective learning is related to the comprehension of the structure of the thematic unit of work the participants acquire, that is to say, the fundamental ideas and their relations.

The effective learning, so, is a comprehensive learning.

The comprehension depends on the effective development and employment of the concepts. The training implies the use of concepts increasingly abstract, many of which can be defined formally.

The comprehension depends on the capacity of weaving a net of interconnections which relates experiences and previous knowledge to the new information.

The effective learning of any information involves necessarily its comprehensive memorization, its location or storage in a more or less wide net of meanings.

This learning of conceptual structures implies the comprehension of the latter, which cannot be obtained thru repetitive learning.

The wider this net of meanings, the larger the capacity of the participant to establish new relations, generating at the same time, new meanings.

It is possible to identify key concepts or ideas in any topic and the facilitators should make sure that they work on these concepts seriously, since they constitute a firm base for the posterior learning. Simply put, once again, we need to "anchor" the acquisition of new knowledge. This can be done thru emotional experiences lived in the OTEL.

It is necessary to relate the comprehensive learning to the characteristics of deep, superficial and strategic approach of learning.

In the deep approach, the intention of the participant goes to the comprehension of the meaning establishing relations with other knowledge and personal experiences, and he analyzes the information and conclusions from the meaning of the materials.

This demands from the participant an implication and a positive interest, a vivid interaction with the contents of the learning.

But this is not the natural situation, not by any means. Historically, learning has been designed with a superficial approach in mind. We understand it is for a very simple reason: the indicators of fulfillment are quite easy to establish, comparisons between students taking advantage of an "indisputable" mathematical basis (the evaluations).

Here, as managers, we face an awkward situation: how can I measure the ability to work in team, to act as a leader, to communicate, for instance?

It is much easier to go for a superficial approach.

In the superficial approach, the intention is centered on the fulfillment of the requirements of the tasks, on the memorization and reproduction of the content, facts or ideas.

There is no implication of the participant, just passiveness in the accomplishment of his task. It is a matter of mechanical and repetitive learning.

With the strategic approach, the participant tries to obtain good qualifications and knows the requirements, procedures of work and systems of evaluation.

The participant shows a more positive attitude in the superficial approach, but it does not reflect the characteristics of the deep learning.

Finally we must mention some colleagues, who propose the following summary of the principal characteristics of each approach:

1. DEEP APPROACH:

- Intention of understanding.
- Strong interaction with the content.
- Relation of new ideas with the previous knowledge
- Relation of concepts with the daily experience.
- Relation of information with conclusions.
- Examination of the logic of the argument.

2. SUPERFICIAL APPROACH

- Intention of fulfilling the requirements of the task.
- Memorizes the information necessary for exercises or examinations
- Faces the task as an external imposition.
- Absence of reflection brings over of intentions or strategy.
- Loose elements without integration.
- Does not distinguish principles from examples.

3. STRATEGIC APPROACH

- Intention of obtaining as high as possible notes.
- Use of previous examinations to predict questions.
- Organizes the time and distributes the effort to obtain better results.
- Assures suitable materials and conditions of study.

We can see that OTEL is focused on strategic learning approach, what we could call self-development learning.

THE PREDEFINED MODELS
AS COGNITIVE BRIDGES

The effective learning facilitates the utilization of the so called predefined models, defined like concepts or initial ideas presented as frames of reference for the new concepts and new relations.

Hereby, the predefined models turn into cognitive bridges between the new contents and the cognitive structure of the participant, which allow a more effective learning.

The following developments show us a concrete form of applying the predefined models in the education.

The models present three phases of activity:
- Presentation of the predefined model.
- Presentation of the task or material of learning.
- Involution of the cognitive organization.

This proves the existing relation between the material of learning and the existing ideas in the participant.

PRESENTATION OF THE MODEL

They can use the following activities:

Clarification of the aims of the session.

Presentation of the model: to give some ideas or properties, to give examples, to contribute to a context, to remember experiences and relevant knowledge related to the subject matter.

PRESENTATION OF THE TRAINING MATERIAL

It can consist of the following:
- To explain the organization of the work.
- To arrange logically the learning process.
- To present the material. (Informative documents, movies, readings, experiments...).
- To promote the cognitive organization
- To have principles to help achieving the integration reconciliation
- To promote a learning of active listening
- To provoke a critical approach

COMPLEMENTARY EXPLANATIONS

The aim of this step is to "anchor" the new material into the already existing cognitive structure. Among the ways the facilitator has for facilitating the reconciliation of the new material with the cognitive structure, we can mention:
- To remember general ideas.
- To ask over the principal properties of the new material.
- To ask over the existing discrepancies in the material.
- To describe the relations between the new material and the concept or terms of reference used while organizing.

The facilitators must know the extent of cognitive capacities which they can try to develop in their participants; they must bear in mind the active and interactive nature of the knowledge and of the comprehension and, finally, the factors which influence the processes for an effective learning.

The fundamental thing is the effective interaction of the participant with the task instead of a merely superficial contact and repetitive learning.

The exploratory approach of the participant depends on the nature of the task in which he is to be compromised.

The perception the participant has of the task is very influenced, explicitly or implicitly, by the communication the facilitator brings over what he wants to teach, by the idea which has been formed by the participant and by his cognitive capacities.

The facilitator must favor an active-exploratory attitude as a way of achieving effective learning.

Construction of knowledge from the personal experience

The situation of learning comes defined basically by its structural components and the interactive dynamics of the same ones.

Among the components of the situation we have to emphasize the participant, the facilitator, the group, the facilities or environment and the thematic content of the session.

The dynamics of the situation include the interactions between the different components which help shaping a specific configuration for the experience of learning.

The implication, definitively, of the participant will be the indicator of the effectiveness and quality of the experience.

The situations of learning allow us developing new structures: new opinions, expectations, models of conduct, and they allow us understanding better the conduct of the participant.

When having spoken about the learning, we are not thinking only about the processing of the information or knowledge.

We refer to the construction of the whole person, in and out of the school, or more precisely, out of the learning place, whatever it is.

It is, therefore, a more global conception, since:

The reality is not defined in "objective" physical terms, but in perceptive and psychological subjective terms.

The reality one can know is his own interpretation of what is real.

The only reality is what each one perceives thru the five senses and the way he understands or interprets it.

To understand the conduct of the participant it is necessary to distinguish the situation which the facilitator or adult sees and the one which exists between the participants, and which constitute their living space.

The "objectivity" is the representation of the situation, as it exists for the individual in a certain moment.

Consequently, a key concept for his comprehension is that of perception and perceptive process, since the behavior of the persons depends on the following three elements:

1. How the person deals with himself.
2. How he sees the situations in which he is immersed.
3. The interrelationships between those two perceptions.

Thru this perceptive process, the person constructs and interprets the external events and the personal experiences, which will lead him to new values and procedures for performance.

This would be the real meaning of the experience of learning.

Inside the effective cognitive learning, an interaction exists between a material and new information with the cognitive structure of the individual. The construction of the meanings, so, is individual.

The construction of meanings implies that the participant, not only in his previous knowledge, develops an aptitude for establishing substantive relations between those previous and the new material; or between the different parts of the learning material of learning.

What do I learn?
How do I learn it?

What's interesting in this kind of learning is that it incorporates important things that exercise transcendent influence on the own conduct, that is, things that should be capable of influencing effectively the conduct.

A person learns effectively those things he perceives they are linked with survival or with the development of his own being.

The brief response to the second question is thru the self-disclosed and self initiated learning which arises from the analysis of the own experiences and from the own questions or needs.

This approach highlights the comprehension of the experience as nucleus of the learning.

In it the person is involved, and there arise one way or another, some thoughts, feelings, attitudes and values, which form new structures of the own personality.

Three characteristics
of the effective learning.

1. Opening to the experience

The individual acquires his capacity for exploring himself and for experiencing what happens in his interior. He is opened to the feelings of fear, despondency, pain, courage, and tenderness. He experiences major confidence in his organism, as a way for reaching the most satisfactory conduct in every existential situation.

The individual is always free to self analyze, and to protect himself behind some "costume". The facilitator should never provoke a debate or a discussion on those topics, as the most likely reaction will be the "clam shell reflex", and we don't have time enough during an OTEL session for individual therapy, nor it is the purpose.

So, the participant decides whether progressing or regressing, behaving in destructive ways for him and the others or adopting new behaviors.

The facilitator is neither a judge nor a prosecutor. His sole concern must be the group. The only thing he cannot allow to happen is that a specific individual contaminates the rest of the group.

That's the only unbreakable rule.

2. Change behavior

The person with his inner structure and organization perceives a situation which will lead him to a change.

Beware: The educational session can appear or be perceived as help for progress, or as a personal threat (always remember the comfort zone).

The education implies a permanent growth, since the individual lives constantly through new experiences he has to incorporate to his own self.

3. Discovery and comprehension

The learning supposes a discovery and comprehension of the environment, and the self-incorporation, that is to say, an effective learning, which answers to the needs and interests of the participant.

The effective OTEL is a learning centered on the participant as "whole" person.

To liberate the curiosity, to allow the persons to evolve according to their own interests, to open everything for questioning and exploring, to admit that everything is in a process of change, though it is never achieved in a total way.

When we say "liberate the curiosity", in fact many times we will have to create it from scratch, or even worse, starting with a negative —and non curious— attitude of the participant.

If we face such a situation, there is no miraculous recipe. We must devote all the required time for this curiosity to "spontaneously" appear.

It is not a major problem if that step requires a drastic change in the tentative timing. We have no other option than dealing with that situation before starting working efficiently. Otherwise, our entire endeavor will prove to be vain.

And, which are the activities most suitable for that purpose? We have compiled for you the activities we normally use, as having proven to be the most effective from our point of view.

Part 4
Some basic OTEL activities

WHICH ACTIVITIES ARE SUITABLE?

Remember that OTEL proposes situations of playful design, using materials like ropes, buckets, balls, pipes or pieces of wood. Actually, any piece of "poor" material.

In order to successfully perform those activities, the participants have:

- To define problems.
- To visualize the result and his consequences.
- To share ideas.
- To take decisions.
- To try alternatives and strategies.
- To acquire confidence.
- To communicate openly.
- To give and to receive feedback.
- To manage the interpersonal and situational diversity.
- To develop the individual contribution.
- To cooperate to reach solutions.

Also remember that every person can always decide his level of participation in every activity. This aspect is vital.

OTEL is not a sports competition. The exercises are not physically demanding. Or they should never be, though viewed from the outside, they could look so.

The development of the program combines these activities with theoretical supports, obtaining high levels of involvement and learning. Systematically they produce opportunities for the overcoming, the change and the improvement.

The facilitators facilitate —obviously— and support the progress of the group.

They do it depending on the specific aims defined for every program with every client.

After every activity, they help the participants consolidating the last step of the pedagogic process, the transference to the working place of the individual and team knowledge.

And what is obtained, in the Short, Mid or Long term?

Can we achieve so many things in just a few days?

Well, let's have a look at some classic activities.

OTEL ACTIVITIES. THE PAPER CAR.

This activity is not of our own creation. Nevertheless, throughout the years, we have contributed with some personal modifications to make it "richer" and quite polyvalent.

It is about building a car, more or less of real size; using only old newspapers (approximately 150 kilos, or 300 pounds), duct tape (approximately 15 rolls) and packing paper (approximately 5 square meters, or 50 square feet). The approximate cost is 50$.

The initial design was thought as an exercise of strengthening team, for groups between 80 and 150 persons. The dimensions of the car were of 2,50x1,50x1,50 meters (8*5*5 feet). The approximate total time for his exercise was of two hours and a half.

Nevertheless, we realized that we could extract some more learning from that activity.

We started experimenting with smaller groups and smaller dimensions. Equally, we realized that it could be a great tool to practice project management and all the collateral skills.

Summarizing, we managed to reduce the dimensions up to the following ones: 1,50x1,00x0,80 meters (5*3*2 feet) with a group of 20 persons, respecting the initial time of two hours and a half. Warning! This time is only the time used in the physical construction of the artifact.

If you use this activity for practicing project management abilities, (planning, budget, follow-up, delivery) you will have to double the initial timing:

Left: Excitation when constructing a car together as a team. It is natural human reflex to start with some skeptical attitude when you are told what is the mission we propose you (building a small car with just old newspapers and duct tape). Nevertheless, as soon as you start assembling the parts, adrenaline flows thru your veins, and you find yourself absorbed in the fulfillment of the task, like if it was a matter of life or death. All of us, human being, have the power to unleash that inner potential strength.

Midle: They all participate, as a real team. Once the car is finished, the feeling of pride, of success, of belonging, and of self-overcoming is overwhelming. The team will remember for a long time what they have achieved today.

Bottom: For large groups, a truck is constructed instead of a car. The framing is the same. The sole difference is in the size of the vehicle, and the number of axles. For technical reasons, the larger the vehicle, the more numerous the axles, for they support the whole body of the car or truck.

On the other hand, because of the new and reduced dimensions, we are no longer limited by the initial design, which forces us to use this activity solely for numerous groups.

That point is relevant, as large groups are not the usual thing, even in big companies. So we need an activity, rich and powerful, but suitable to a standard group size (around 20 people). The paper car is quite OK. The material is easy to find; rag pickers being our usual suppliers. Just don't use material too spoiled. One thing is working with "poor" material; another thing is dealing with garbage.

THE PAPER BRIDGE

Engineering the bridge. With great care, as they will have to cross it. The height –from ground level– should be of about one meter. Beware of the security aspects, as we do not use any security appliance, like helmets or harnesses and ropes. We are the safety structure.

This OTEL activity is entirely of our own design, and can be a support for virtually any "soft skill".

But let's not forget that the activity itself IS NOT the training. The activity is just a way for leading us to a more or less rich debriefing.

When I designed this activity, as far back as the year 1.997, I wanted to reach the Holy Grail, namely an activity which allowed us practicing and developing all of the concepts of the OTEL.

First of all let's briefly see what is the activity about:

The material we will use is:

- Rope of hemp of 8 mm (1/4 inch). Approximately one hundred meters (100 yards). It is important not to use nylon climbing ropes. The material has to look awkward and fragile.
- Old newspapers, approximately 50 kilos (100 pounds).
- Duct tape, approximately ten rolls.

The approximate total cost is of 70$.

The participants, with a few imprecise instructions, have to construct a "monkey bridge". As soon as they have constructed the above-mentioned bridge, they must cross it.

We can see that the approach turns out to be very simple; nevertheless, in the briefing we raise the following reflections and metaphors.

- With some poor materials (this is what we have, as in real life).
- You have to design a bridge (how translating a vague concept into a reality).
- The instructions are poor, or incomplete ... (creativity).
- You have to do it in team (how to form team).
- Who is to be the Director of the project (leadership)?

Top: They all are responsible for the bridge to resist the weight of the participants. With great pride, they pose in front of it.
Bottom: Remember the material has to be poor...

- Since this construction consists of several elements, there will be specialized groups who will have to work together, and synchronized for the final assembly, (this is a project management activity).
- The material is not free (nothing is for free in this life) and it is necessary to manage it as best as possible.
- Once constructed, you will have to cross it (demonstrating the confidence in your own skill).
- There are neither harnesses nor helmets (you will be responsible for the safety of the colleagues who cross).
- When the first one has crossed over (quality checking and safety), do not relax (routine is a great threat for the organizations).
- You can, if you want, ask your facilitator to cross it (in this case the facilitator will be your client. If you convince him, then he will cross).
- Etc...

So summarizing, we can see that, depending on the needs, it is possible to insist on one or other one of the facets you would want to be emphasized.

So far, from my point of view, this exercise (because of its low cost, as the ropes can be returned to be used in a posterior session), has, from my point of view, the best relation in terms of ratio simplicity / cost / result.

Only one vital logistics parameter has to be taken in account. It is necessary to have trees of strong and sturdy trunk (a diameter of more than 20 cm), not too distant (5 or 6 meters), to be able to support the bridge.

Though in some occasion, it was constructed "Indoor", actually the mechanical workshop of a huge cars retailer, for an international prestige brand, —hanging the bridge from two pillars of concrete—, this is not the usual location.

So finally, if you can meet the above-mentioned conditions, I eagerly recommend you experiment with the Bridge of Paper.

FREEFALL OF THE EGG

The team has to construct an appliance which will prevent the egg to be broken. They have to buy the material in a fictitious shop. The egg is obviously not boiled.

This exercise, which some engineers schools have incorporated as a graduation playful activity is actually more complex, if we want to extract the whole juice. In our approach, it is not any contest.

The briefing of the exercise.

Every team has to decide of a profit objective of free fall (in centimeters). For each ten centimeters (3 inches) they earn 1$.

To prevent the breaking of the egg, they construct an appliance with the following material:

- Drinking straws.
- Meters of painters tape (narrow, no more than an inch wide)
- Small elastic bands

EACH ELEMENT COSTS THEM 1$

As soon as the appliance has been constructed, we proceed to the testing step.

The metaphor is "The egg is the client". The fall height of the egg is a Moment of Truth. The Egg breaks, or does not break. There is no possible excuse or alibi.

The profit of the whole operation is the difference between the fall and the cost of the bought material.

This one is a Moment of the Truth. The egg breaks or does not break. There are no alternatives.

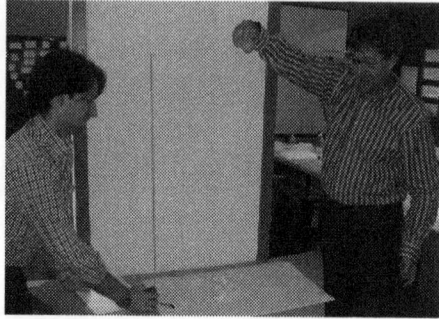

The whole team is responsible for the result. You may invest little and then pray for the egg not to break. But, if you wish, you may invest a lot for a small payback, whatever.

What's important is that you are responsible for the final outcome.

This exercise also helps stretching bonds in a team, creating an environment of competition. It is one of the very few OTEL activities where we introduce the factor competition.

Other classic exercises

We can define three types of OTEL activities, sorting them by places of realization, instead of by type of activity.

These only are some examples of the most widely experienced; though many others exist, and more of them are being designed every day.

The differentiation is:

1. Pure Outdoor

Activities which must take place only in open field. Besides, many of these activities need the presence of trees.

2. Mixed activities

Depending on availabilities of space, we can choose to develop them one way or another.

3. Pure Indoor

Activities only to be developed indoors, because we need a protected or covered area, a flat area, even tables.

1. Pure Outdoor

The ski race

The ropes have been fixed to the boards so the participants must give all the walking steps synchronized.

It is possible to do this exercise indoor, but for safety reasons, it is not recommended (falls and frets)

This is a very exciting –and funny– race

The team radar

The team (with bandaged eyes) has to reach a previously selected target (normally a tree).

What happens when we leave our comfort zone and face such a peculiar challenge? We are "blind" and we must establish new rules, new behaviors if we want to "survive" that exercise.

Rappel

In a rocky wall, or descending from a bridge, classical individual rappel. If you want to complicate things, you can tie the participants to each other.

A classic outdoors activity. Not very demanding physically but tending to be somewhat binary. Recommended for being used towards the end of a program, when people have already been experiencing their move out of their comfort zone.

The wall

There, it is necessary to climb as high as possible, but the participants are tied together.

The post

A post approximately 8 meters (25 feet) high with a small platform on top. It is necessary to climb as high as possible, exploring the limits of the comfort zone and then jump (although this is not mandatory, remember it is *not* a contest).

The most powerful exercise of exploration of the limits of the comfort zone. Complex infrastructure required. Only in a very professionally controlled environment.

Powerful exercise, but it needs a heavy infrastructure. It is advisable to use a climbing wall, instead of natural rocks, for reasons of safety and to avoid small –although painful– injuries.

The high wire

Complex infrastructure required. Only in a very professionally controlled environment.

Gangplank

The challenge is to cross thru the gangplank without any help and then return to the starting point.

Trust fall

To create confidence is only one of the applications of this classic and very widely spread activity.

It is necessary to do it with some precaution. This activity needs to dedicate a lot of care to the safety issues.

People have to walk on the wires, for an intense meeting at the confluence. The last step of the trip has to be performed together. No other option. On the picture, the author, tensing the wires, prepares the coming exercise.

The classic one. Very powerful. It does not require any material. Very demanding in terms of safety procedures, both for the "faller", and for the rest of the team, in charge of the smooth reception of the "faller".

Heavy infrastructure. Only in controlled environment. To be used as a complementary exercise.

A more complex and complete activity than it looks. We recommend it always when possible; the debriefing can be very rich. The only safety attachments are the helmets (indispensable).

The Low V

Two tensed cables shaping a V –about one meter above the ground– is everything needed for this activity.

The dynamics of teams and systems are some of the learning points of this activity.

The Spider Web

The whole team must cross the spider web. It seems easy, but will they be able to do it without touching the net?

Basic activity of the Outdoor, to involve a large group. It is an excellent closing exercise. The record is of 200 participants at the same time.

OTHER CLASSIC ACTIVITIES

The Platform (variant of the Post)

A platform of 0,16 m2 (one square foot). Suspended in the air at 7 meters (20 feet) of height. The only access is a stairs of rope. Not only it supposes a personal challenge but a task for the whole team.

Orientation

Identifiable signs the participants must locate in order to reach the final target.

Road of orientation

By means of a map, the participants must locate a few points identified by a few beacons.

Triangle

Between 3 trees we tie a rope tensed in such a way that it forms an equilateral triangle. They have to pass over the rope helped by their colleagues and without touching the ground. It is a variant of the web.

Sloping trunk

The challenge is to climb on a sloping telegraph pole.

It is possible to use any technique or idea providing it is not dangerous

Cooperative step

Between 2 trees a rope is tied, and above this one another rope without tensing. Similar to the gangplank, but with less height and infrastructure. It is a matter of crossing to the other side.

Steps of giant

A few tables and a few ropes are facilitated to the participants. It is a question of realizing a tour between a few cones using these means without treading on the ground and helped by his colleagues.

Tower of boxes

Constructing an evolving structure of plastic boxes with two members of the team in balance on them.

How much high will they be able to go?

Weismuller (also known as Tarzan)

A cable in tension and a series of vines provide a challenge which goes in increase since the vines are increasingly separated. You must leap from one vine to another

Discs

The items are sold to all the participants except to two. It is a question of locating a few previously hidden discs.

Blind team

The items are sold to all the participants and several chunks of rope are distributed on the ground. It is necessary to locate these ropes and realize with them a geometric figure.

America's Cup (complex and expensive)

The participants, in teams, will learn to man a sailboat, to attend to the orders of the captain and to solve adverse situations. Quiet powerful, although obviously expensive and requiring some heavy logistics.

Shipwrecked persons

The participants, who are forming two teams, are distributed by different places and, by means of walkie-talkies, must coordinate themselves and construct a raft. Once built, they will sail up to finding a capsule with part of a manuscript, then, they'll have to meet another team and complete the message.

The Giant Stairs

These stairs measures 8 meters (25 feet) in height. It is it sufficiently broad for 2 persons to climb it simultaneously. The difficulty is in the distance between the steps, as they go more and more separated from each other. Beware, it may prove to be some quite physically demanding exercise if people feel too excited.

2. Mixed activities (indoor/outdoor)

Canvas

A canvas is placed on the ground and the group on the canvas. They have to turn the canvas upside down while the group keeps standing on top of it and not treading on the bare floor.

The archipelago

Variant of the previous one. The participants distribute in groups of three, each one on an "island". They have to turn them upside down without treading on the "water".

Rescuing the client

The client is symbolized by a glass full of water, entrapped in a dead zone, where no living being can enter (like if there were a glass wall).

An excellent exercise for the indoor.

Very simple, but very effective. Perfect for indoor as well as for outdoors.

The team has to construct an appliance which will allow them "to "rescue" the client. Those who handle the appliance wear the bandana.

They can use strings and rubber bands.

The blind polygon

Bandaged, it is necessary to construct a geometric figure with one rope. The whole group –blinded– holds the rope. Then you give them instructions, and the whole group has to come to an organizational structure which will allow them communicating and reaching an agreement, prior to laying the rope on the ground.

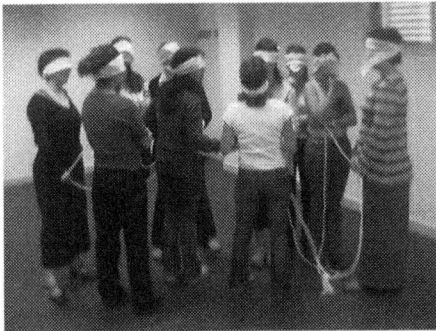

How difficult it is to coordinate a team when we are blinded and we lose our non-verbal capacity.

Diamonds

Positions are distributed in the group. Three workmen, two managers and the director. The director has to organize the personnel in such a way that manipulating a mechanism can help them recovering a few diamonds distributed by a square.

3. Indoor

The labyrinth

It's a classical, albeit powerful indoor exercise.

In a rectangle of 48 cells, more or less similar to a chessboard, there is only one path for crossing. Every failure bears penalty. The exercise itself has to be done silently.

The size of the maze can be of about 4 * 3 meters. The trick is that the path we choose has to be erratic (never straightforward).

The idea is to experiment what happens when we reach a dead end, and get stuck trying to walk forward, when it becomes obvious that we have to step back and then try again, looking for soft spots in the maze.

X					
	X		X		
X			X		X
X		X			X
	X				X
					X
				X	
					X

Quite intellectual exercise, but look at the
puzzled faces of the participants, trying
to reach a conclusion and to perform
according to the previous tentative
commitment they supposedly had reached.

We allow the participants 15 minutes to design a strategy.
When they are ready to start, silence is compulsory during the
whole exercise.

Penalties and rewards. If they cross in 15 minutes, they get
15.000 $. Each minute overtime bears a penalty of 1.000 $. If
they stomp on a wrong cell, we blow the whistle and compute
a penalty of 500$, and they must go back till the departing
point, using the same path as on the going route. Whenever
they stomp on a forbidden cell, penalty occurs.

At the end of the exercise, when all of the participants have
crossed, we make the final computing of results. Normally,
they end up losing money.

It is a very frustrating exercise, albeit rich of learnings.

Learnings about planning, time management, communication, resources management, quality control, strategic aims,
team work, etc …

Actually, it reminds us of real life, as all the OTEL does.

Part 5
Conclusions

OTEL Education

Closing the loop, we now must summarize all of the aspects of the OTEL.

Let's start with the most visual aspect of OTEL, the physical activity and its impact. Put in other words, why, whatever the ability of the facilitator and the design of the activities, the OTEL always works, one way or another.

Or, at least, why it never fails. But beware; there is anyway one requisite, and it the respect of the Decalogue.

If we do not respect it, then the results can be extremely negative. So let's have a final overall look at the concepts of OTEL.

We have some friends and colleagues (or mere acquaintances) who have studied in centers of great prestige, as we all have done, and nevertheless, find themselves marooned in a dusty and smelly office, or occupying positions and functions of a category much lower than what they might be supposed to dream of.

In fact, they are castaways in extremely technical positions, where they have small or no interaction with others.

Has this something to do with the form in which they have received their education?

Please notice: Here, at the moment we do not consider the inherent cost of applying OTEL methodologies in order to favor the acquisition of knowledge and skills.

Sadly, such a cost exists, although it is hidden. A very simple example: to work with OTEL methodologies, I cannot have just a single facilitator for 30 or 40 participants (or pupils, or students, you name it). I need a facilitator –besides being a specialist of OTEL– for each dozen of participants. It means that I need three times more facilitators, with the cost it represents.

The debate –we do not want to enter here– is about knowing if it compensates to form the whole world in a "bad way", in order that they at least "learn something", or if I aim at an elitist model where I assume that only a small privileged percentage of people will receive select education.

Here we are facing a debate about some model of society, but this not the object of this book. Simply, to liquidate the matter, just say that, albeit in a veiled form, this is what has been happening for centuries. Just remember that Alexander the Great had as a particular facilitator no less than Aristotle. I guess it helps achieving great success!

The problem is that the standard elite is not an intellectual elite, it is a wealth elite. So the society dedicates huge resources to train people who will not optimize the education they receive (well, Alexander optimized it, and optimized it well, but it's not what you usually expect...)

This is another debate. The pragmatic question here and today is: Can I, with a cost not turning out to be prohibitive, integrate more efficient methodologies –not simply linear– into the basic education?

We want –I suppose– to give a good education to our children and teenagers, the generation of our future. An integral education of the whole person. And all the countries have developed systems of education, more or less efficient.

When saying that, you may notice that we are just extrapolating what we said about companies and competence; applying it to the development of a whole country and / or model of society and development.

Nevertheless, we think that the basics remain the same; despite what some economists friends of mine would object.

Actually, there is a constant which self repeats in all the systems, and it is that merely intellectual activities develop just analytical linear skills; when our brain is a magnificent parallel processor but a depressing linear processor (any calculator worth 5 $ obtains better and more rapid results than the major genius of mathematics).

But actually, what does happen?

The educational official system is a system thought almost only for the brain. More than twenty weekly hours are academic matters of theory and mental learning. In the educational system, the concept of the man is reduced to his mere brain. But educating only the brain and forgetting about the whole man as an integral and total person may produce some unexpected outcomes (remember my brilliant colleagues, stuck in dull positions).

The body, the corporal, emotional, social, compensatory needs etc. They have neither importance nor systematical place in the study or in the school / institutional life. What counts is the academic learning, the discipline, an order well constructed in the classes, to avoid interruptions, disturbances or problems in the class etc.

Schools are understood as factories of academic education. They are determined by the efficiency of the academic learning.

Scarcely there takes place any social or emotional learning, almost nothing of systematical training in the corporal, sexual area etc. There are no information about the managing of the own personality, the skills of communication and solution of interpersonal problems, the psycho ruling against the aggression and violence etc.

The educational system imposes a great quantity of matters of study to participants, gathered, or sometimes packed in great quantity in classrooms. This increases stress, frustrations and then aggressions and violence in case of not fulfilling the expectations (what normally happens, by the way).

Another, and not irrelevant point; when talking about students. Normally, the participants or students continue working or studying in a strict seating position for days, weeks, months, years, and decades. Six hours or more everyday day; and then, later in the evening, they continue with their tasks, computer, television, eaten, always seated. Pretty bad.

In many houses, the dogs, horses or other domestic animals have more physical activity than the children, because it is known that otherwise the animals have corporal or health problems.

This sedentary life has its price: the lack of movement with the consequences of " mechanical failures " of the body as cardiovascular, muscular problems, of the metabolism, of growth, of weight, of the column, of position in general, psychophysical problems in base of adrenalines, endorphins etc.

The child in process of growth does not receive his physiological impulses necessary for the natural and corporal development. Negative and serious consequences to the suitable development of the intelligence already are scientifically verified. And more or less the same applies to us adults.

MOVEMENT AND BRAIN.
FUNCTIONS, MECHANISMS
AND CONSEQUENCES

What are the confirmed scientific results with reference to the interrelationships between movement and cerebral activities? And, eventually, one of the explanations of why OTEL naturally work.

In the physiopsychology there are already large investigations with very effective results on the effects of the movement in the activities of the brain of the human being:

Movement enlivens the mechanisms of metabolism producing hormones and products of metabolism (endorphins etc.). They improve the body well-being and the mental attention.

More movement could deplete too much the level of hormones and endorphins in the organic system. Bear in mind that those levels cannot be diminished practicing video or viewing violent movies. We miss the movement and thus the physically efficient activity.

Movement activates certain cerebral regions: Cortex, ganglions, cerebellum, that is to say centers necessary for the learning activity, both cognitive and social knowledge. This one is another added facet of the OTEL.

Movement increases the contacts and the development of synapses in certain cerebral regions. For example the children who do not move over 30 % of their normal capacity stop the development of their intelligence.

The physical activity improves the function of the brain: An average level of activation is the ideal one. The movement is an activator in an average level and a desactivador in a too high level. Less than 30 % is not effective.

Movement normalizes and improves coordination: The children who watch TV more than 2 hours a day develop a co-ordination worse than those who do not. And besides, they discover some not so enlightening aspects of life in our world of adults. (But that's another story altogether…)

Movement reduces the level of aggressiveness thanks to the consumption of hormones generating stress.

The movement increases the well being as:

- It reduces the distress and panic (current and/or chronic).
- It increases the conscience of the own corporal skill: Indicator for the feeling of the corporal and psychic well-being.
- It reduces the reaction to social stress.
- It improves the reactions in cases like stumbles or falls.
- It improves reaction in cases of depressive symptoms.
- It increases the resistance to the overcharge.
- The movement serves like a psycho regulator

Besides we have one of the basic rules of life, suitable for infantile as well as for adults: the one who does not move puts on weight and falls ill. (Brilliant, isn't it?)

Obviously, things are not always that easy, but it gives us a hint about how the mere movement and action can be an energizer (definitely) and a tool for the acquisition of learning.

This rule suits for all the living beings in the world and it is necessary to know or learn it, better when one is young, so you can remember once you are an adult, working in a company.

Definitively, because of the support of movement, what we see is that OTEL is a self-supporting methodology.

Therefore, any program Outdoor –even poorly made– will produce results, because in its process are enclosed the results.

Here, a sentence from one of my preferred masters –Steve Webster, to whom we all owe so much– a sentence which has helped me in so many occasions, specially when having to deal with difficult groups: "Trust the process".

The OTEL process works by itself. The mere accomplishment of "playful" activities produces results. That these are more or less impacting, practical and long lasting, it depends on the talent of the designers and facilitators of the activities.

CONCLUSIONS.
A METHODOLOGY WITH RESULTS

As a conclusion, we must have in mind that when we are doing OTEL, we are talking about three horizons.

1. IMMEDIATE

The program proves to be motivating, challenging and entertaining. The look on the faces of the participants demonstrates it. In the moment of the evaluation, satisfaction shows on the people, just because of the singularity and the power of the methodology.

2. IN THE MID TERM

The thought "beyond the common" which is stimulated by the activities, reinforces the enthusiasm, improves the communication and the feedback and encourages the creativity. The participants develop new or refined attitudes and skills, producing invariably a real impact on the way they act when returning to the workplace.

3. LONG TERM

The OTEL turns us into an architect of the change of behavior towards the collaboration, the confidence, the efficiency and the performance.

Additionally, being in the outdoors, and living a different experience, helps the participants constructing situations and experiences which will remain in their minds and hearts for a lot of time, and besides —another interesting aspect— it will happen to form a part of the collective memory of the organizations.

DON'T FORGET
THESE POINTS ABOUT OTEL

Now, we clearly understand that in a market increasingly competitive and increasingly focused on the client, the competitive factor is the people within my organization.

So why don't we start, once and for all, working on the acquisition of those techniques?

Nowadays, for the success of the organizations and the competitive differentiation it is necessary to manage adequately the soft capital, namely the talent, creativity, intelligence, aspirations and motivations of the personnel of a company, framed inside a culture organizational which allows answering with agility to the permanent requirements of the modern world.

Let's remember again Confucius: (besides it has been scientifically verified, even recently by my friends from Milton Keynes Open University): we learn 20 % of what we listen, 40 % of what we see and hear and 80 % of what we do.

This proves that the existential experience opposite to classroom courses or traditional conferences typical of managerial trainings is much richer and effective. Here it is when the system of training of OTEL unveils its importance.

Never forgetting that OTEL is somehow a technique or alternative tool using concepts linked to "the military thing" in order to design strategies which foment the relations between civil servants or managers in order to improve their productivity.

It is also a tool for resolution of conflicts or improvement of already existing teams.

The OTEL presents a logical sequence of activities where there are extracted conclusions which help to improve the personal and professional environment.

That's another point we tend to forget. An OTEL session is like a movie, with its actors, their directors, and the script. There is a certain pace; we must not break that pace. The movie has to be logical, each activity smoothly linking to the next in line, to give a final and clear message.

Designed specially for small teams of professionals, these courses combine OTEL activities with meetings for reflection which promote, thru the practice and the experience, the change in the way of thinking and acting of the participants, affecting in those aspects of the group which are necessary to reinforce: leadership, taking of decisions, team work, personal development, etc.

In a formative session which rests on an experimental learning, the participants organized in teams, will have to overcome several exercises related to four elements of the nature: fire, water, land and air, and they will exercise the two factors key to achieve the success: the competitiveness between the teams and the coordination within them.

These activities are designed for promoting skills such as:
- Communication
- Motivation
- Team work

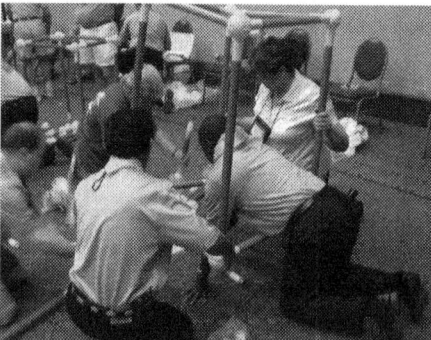

The important thing is the fact of constructing something; it is not so much the final result. This activity can be outdoors or indoors, depending on the weather.

- Colleagueship
- Self confidence and Creativity
- Management of Time and Change
- Spirit of overcoming
- Leadership

Although, as you now see, this list is not self-limiting. Once we have really understood how and when we can use OTEL, we can think of many other skills to be developed or reinforced used that methodology. You establish the limits.

FINAL ADVICES

At the end, we can summarize OTEL in a few sentences:

a. The OTEL sessions are developed outdoors (or in classroom, let's never forget it, it is also OTEL), in a context of high informality, which favors the appearance of behaviors which normally do not arise in more conventional environments.

b. The central aim is to foment and to develop the professional skills which allow the persons to be employed more effectively in his company. Never ever forget about that; we will go on repeating this statement forever and ever.

c. For it works on the physical and the emotional facets, promoting a high degree of involvement, participation and enthusiasm.

d. They promote skills of communication, reinforce the colleagueship, and support the self-confidence, the creativity and the spirit of overcoming.

e. It is a matter of creating, based on an academic pre-established plan, real experiences which allow the members of a company or organization, to combine talents and to face effective and efficient actions.

f. It is training oriented to practice and to existential, where the important thing is the experiences of the person and the group in the context of the program. It is a question of putting the persons in front of new challenges in order that they develop their aptitude to act.

g. The individuals are lead to reach a major spirit of team and sense of belonging.

h. The development of skills, change of behavior and involution of the work in team, team building, is realized by exercises and real experiences, in which the persons, out of the daily job environment and in touch with the nature, discover many positive facets of behavior.

i. It is a question of "memorable" activities, of high emotional impact, which allow to fix and to retain concepts which support the professional management in the organizations.

j. They are days of intense work, which allow us to obtain concrete results in the persons and organizations.

k. They offer experiences to the attendees in order that they extract conclusions on what they have seen or heard.

l. It raises exercises and challenges which move the participants away from their comfort zone, generating a learning from the experience, with a high capacity of retention and persistence of conducts.

m. The activity developed outdoors (or in classroom, in an informal environment) implies movements, creativity, ingenuity and physical energy.

n. Any member of the company or organization can take part. It is not necessary to be an athlete to participate.

o. But, be careful, if there is a positive predisposition and spirit of adventure, we are not going out of the comfort zone, and we are not learning anything.

p. The schemes of OTEL are basically orientated to promote the cohesion of teams, to strengthen the feelings of belonging, to support the leadership, to solve conflicts, to improve the levels of interpersonal communication, to stimulate the creativity and the taking of decisions.

q. It doesn't seem wise to use OTEL for therapeutic purposes, unless under strict and top class supervision.

Let's take a final classic example, in order to consolidate all the concepts. In this supposition, the script has to deal with explorers.

We organize some explorers expedition who have to look for a land of great symbolic value, where to construct all together a new city (actually a camp).

The construction of a camp will be the common objective of the participants. The program of OTEL has to promote the internal communication, using the taking of decisions and the work at team.

In order to raise expectations before the action, and simultaneously involving all the participants, fomenting a positive attitude towards the training, we send a communiqué informing them about their mission: to construct a city, or a camp.

The distribution of functions and tasks, the leadership style, the work in team, the resolution of conflicts, the taking of decisions, the planning, the quantity and quality of results and the communication are factors to observe and promote during the OTEL activity outdoor.

Later, this session was reinforced and complemented by a formative session in classroom where it was thought over some troubled or representative situations.

Here are some of the outcomes. Here are reflected most of the skills we can develop thru OTEL.

Organizational development	Human development
Management of the Change	Emotional intelligence
Mission and Organizational Vision	Change of Attitude
Direction for Values	Management and Leadership
Climate and Managerial Culture	Self motivation
Systems of Communication	Management of the Stress
Management of the Knowledge	Negotiation and Management of Conflicts
Management of Skills	Team work
Evaluation of the human Potential.	Time Management
Marketing and Sales	Direction of Meetings
Quality and Attention to the Client.	Interpersonal communication
Organization and Systems	Effective presentations
Facilitators training	Creative thinking

Final message

Finally, after our trip thru many aspects of the OTEL, we can say that the only vital rules, from our point of view, are embedded in the Decalogue. If you respect the enclosed points, you will be successful; we have no doubt about it.

And what about us?

Personally, always respecting our Decalogue, we will continue developing programs and exploring new applications of the OTEL methodology. There is still a lot to be developed in this exciting world.

But now it is your turn to move out of your Comfort Zone and to put into practice and experience OTEL.

And finally, once again, don't forget what Steven Webster said about OTEL: "Trust the Process. It works"

LibrosEnRed Publishing House

LibrosEnRed is the most complete digital publishing house in the Spanish language. Since June 2000 we have published and sold digital and printed-on-demand books.

Our mission is to help all authors publish their work and offer the readers fast and economic access to all types of books.

We publish novels, stories, poems, research theses, manuals, and monographs. We cover a wide range of contents. We offer the possibility to commercialize and promote new titles through the Internet to millions of potential readers.

Our royalties system allows authors to receive a profit 300% to 400% greater than they would obtain in the traditional circuit.

Enter www.librosenred.com to see our catalog, comprising of hundreds of classic titles and contemporary authors.